FARSCAPE™

THE ILLUSTRATED SEASON 3 COMPANION

FARSCAPE: THE ILLUSTRATED SEASON 3 COMPANION

1 84023 415 6

Published by
Titan Books
A division of
Titan Publishing Group Ltd
144 Southwark St
London
SE1 0UP

First edition June 2002
2 4 6 8 10 9 7 5 3

Photographs supplied by The Jim Henson Company, *Farscape* Productions, Yoram Gross-E.M.-TV Studios and Ruth Thomas.

ACKNOWLEDGEMENTS

The authors would like to thank the following for their help in preparing this book: all of those we interviewed for so graciously giving up their time; Lily Taylor, Paula Jensen and Emanda Thomas on the *Farscape* set, Fiona Searson at DDA Australia and Dan Bateman at Henson's, London for their help in setting up the interviews; Sinead Bennett, Katrina Gerhard and Tony Tatman for their help in the preparation of the manuscript; Adam Newell, David Barraclough, Jo Boylett and Oz Browne at Titan; and especially Rockne S. O'Bannon and David Kemper for yet again being available for questions and discussion despite the many other calls on their time.

DEDICATION

To Jenn Fletcher, my first companion in the Uncharted Territories of Hollywood — PS.

To my dad, for encouraging me to stay up late on Friday nights and discover the weird and wonderful world of Science Fiction — RT.

Did you enjoy this book? We love to hear from our readers.
Please e-mail us at: readerfeedback@titanemail.com or write to Reader Feedback at the above address.
To subscribe to our regular newsletter for up-to-the-minute news, great offers and competitions,
email: titan-news@titanemail.com

Titan Books' film and TV range, including the *Farscape Illustrated Companion* series, are available from all good bookshops or direct from our mail order service. For a free catalogue or to order, phone 01536 764646 with your credit card details, or write to Titan Books Mail Order, AASM Ltd, Unit 6, Pipewell Industrial Estate, Desborough, Northants, NN14 2SW. Please quote reference FS/C3.

A CIP catalogue record for this title is available from the British Library.

Printed and bound in Great Britain by MPG, Bodmin, Cornwall.

FARSCAPE™

THE ILLUSTRATED SEASON 3 COMPANION

Paul Simpson and Ruth Thomas

Series created by Rockne S. O'Bannon

TITAN BOOKS

CONTENTS

o, you've got yourself a *Farscape* book. Congratulations. And Happy Birthday! (No one buys this kind of book for themselves.) This is the first Foreword I've ever been asked to write, and almost certainly, the last. I lobbied hard for the 'Backword' to the book, but Paul and Ruth were adamant. Foreword only. (My logic is, who wants to read something at the *start* of a book that isn't even by the damn authors? I don't. I wanna get to the good stuff. But at the *end* of a great book, you always want more. See, that's the Backword. You're so desperate for additional material, you'll even read something by *me*.)

Anyway, this is a good book to get as a gift. I have known and trusted Paul and Ruth for years. They talk to everybody, come to the set, and diligently research things. This means that most of the stuff they write is actually true. (Unlike *some* noted historians of late, who just rip off other writers. That would be like our writing team remembering a classic episode of a classic sci-fi series and then writing something similar that twisted off *Farscape*-style into a newer version of... Okay, bad example. That's called 'homage'. Look it up. My conscience is clear.)

Before we get into the business of season three, allow me to introduce two people whose names might mean something to you. They're the reason *Farscape* exists, and that this book was written.

Rockne S. O'Bannon. (It should not be hard to grasp that parents who would bestow 'Rockne' as a first name would be unashamed to give 'Stupendous' as a middle.) Rock must now be considered a Titan (clever use of the publisher's name, including a capitalisation, augurs that I will perhaps someday write another book Foreword!) and has created a number of science fiction franchises; all varied, all timeless. *Alien Nation. seaQuest.* Oh, yeah, and *Farscape*. Ask the person who bought you this book. They'll know. Rock's creative mind awes me, and he's my best friend. You'd think I'd be used to it after seventeen years. Anyway, I am enormously proud that I was the first person Rock hired way back in early 1994. Among other things, I owe him the best experience of my life. Everyone else owes him *Farscape*.

Brian Henson. He runs some company that has something to do with *Farscape*. I'm not sure. But Brian has been a friend, confidant, advisor, generous spirit and creative talent beyond expectation. Even his whispers carry great weight on this show. His vision and knowledge combine to reach far forward, constantly creating new creatures, stories, ideas. Remember, it was Brian who called Rockne in 1993 and said, in essence, 'I wanna make a TV show set in space...' Head bow to Brian. (And the offers for Forewords begin to mount up.)

(Okay, now here's the really tricky part. I'm *supposed* to say something insightful about Season 3. But what?! If I write things that are discussed elsewhere in the book, I look stupid and you'll get bored. But if I write cool stuff the authors don't know about, doesn't that make them look uninformed?

They suggested I acknowledge my position as Executive Producer of Farscape to impart an overview of what we tried to do this year. I'd rather continue mentioning people who might one day write books themselves and so consider me for... What the hell, it's their book.)

The third season of this show damn near killed everyone who worked on it. *Apocalypse Farscape*. Our set caught fire and burned down. The dead came back to life and the living suddenly faltered. We lost an extremely valued and irreplaceable member of our cast essentially due to the world's worst ongoing bad-blue-hair day ever. Our lead character was 'twinned' — split into two equal beings — for half the season. One of them fell in love. And then he died. Everyone cried. We messed with timelines; twisted convention. We packed the screen with humour and anger, usually at the same exact instant. Emotions always ran high. We made a cartoon. Our characters screwed up. Lots. Someone met their long-lost mother, then watched her fall away forever. New characters emerged, others flew off. Our original villain completed his metamorphosis to hero, then saved the lives of his once mortal enemy and the woman they both loved. The son of our ship (*those* five words should cause non-viewers standing in the bookstore to gently replace this volume on the shelf) showed more enterprise than any vessel before him. Our lead actor wrote a script; every word of it himself. We learned about our current villain's horrific origins. One character contemplated suicide, and we felt for her. The lambs and the lions lay down together, an uneasy truce, never what it seemed.

New threats emerged; old hatreds rekindled. We watched a wedding that never was, and saw a man dissolve under the weight of his own over-reaching, laid low and alone, without hope.

The old joke goes: and that was just *behind the scenes*.

What we tried to do amidst all that was construct the best series we could. Period. Our mandate has always been More Better Faster. Creative Darwinism — the best idea survives. Friendly competition not to *best* one another, but to *aid* each other in producing something that makes even our jaded group of international film-makers sit back for a moment and go, 'Damn, did we do *that*?' Can we actually split our lead character in two and sustain it for *half a year*? Is it possible to make an episode of television on budget that combines live action, full scenes of computer generated graphics, high gloss cartoon animation, any number of combinations of the above, *and* puppetry — not to mention spacewalks and dream sequences? (The answer is 'no' to the budget part.)

The only way you can tackle a challenge that big is by being unafraid. And the only way to lose your fear in the crucible of television production is by working together. So as you listen to the unafraid stories that follow, keep an ear out for the real secret behind *Farscape*'s success. Collaboration.

It is mostly about "we", "us", "teamwork". Pay attention to the number of times people answer a question by pointing a laudatory finger in someone else's direction. Notice how a problem is often solved from a totally different, and often surprising, quarter. See if you can't sense the respect and esteem the film-makers working on *Farscape* have for one another.

What's not remarkable is that this sort of thing happens in the pressure-cooked world of television. What *is* remarkable is that in such an ego-driven environment, people willingly share their acknowledgement and admiration for others' contributions. And what's *astoundingly* remarkable is that every word of it is heartfelt and true.

The people making *Farscape* are extraordinarily dedicated, uncommonly talented, close-knit as a family, and deeply driven to produce the best television show they can. It's fitting that much of what follows is told in their voices. They're the reason someone bought you this book.

So sit back, enjoy the read, look for the Backword, and have a Happy Birthday!

David Kemper
Sydney, Australia
March 2002

Opposite page:
David Kemper watches calmly as 'Apocalypse Farscape' comes together.

Rockne S. O'Bannon

" We knew we had to spin the show somewhere else, and *Farscape* very appropriately took quite a turn in season three..."

INT. SURGERY ROOM

SCORPIUS

You have cost me much, and I do not suffer disappointment well... I condemn you to <u>live</u>, John Crichton, so that the thirst for unfulfilled revenge may consume you. (Rising, with finality)
Goodbye.

And as Scorpius EXITS, PUSH CLOSE on Crichton, helplessly thrashing, arms and legs bound, secured to the table by his head, brain open and <u>incomplete</u>, eyes on fire, mouth twisted in fury, ANIMALISTIC GRUNTS AND NOISES spilling out!

THE END OF SEASON TWO

The producers of *Farscape* knew that they would be returning to their base at Homebush Bay in November 2000, for the start of the third year. However, during the hiatus following season two, it became clear that not all of the cast would be joining them for the whole of the third season.

Virginia Hey, who had become globally recognised as Pa'u Zotoh Zhaan, was finding the extensive make-up that came with her role increasingly wearing. "As we were shooting 'Die Me, Dichotomy', she was saying that she couldn't do this for another year," executive producer David Kemper recalls. Accordingly he planned that the cost of Aeryn's resurrection would be Zhaan's health and to recuperate, she would need to be planted in the ground. In reality, that meant "Virginia would have some episodes off to regrow her hair, then we would come back and find her, and whatever her hair looked like in real life was what we would use in the show," he explains. However Hey's agent then stated that the actress wanted a reduced workload, but "her requests were not do-able for a television production," Kemper points out.

Hey decided that she would not return. "I tried a thousand ways to talk her out of it, but she was adamant," Kemper says. "Virginia wasn't going to come back at all, but I called her and said, 'Do the character a service. I'll write you a great ending, but you've got to do four full episodes.'"

The decision to write Zhaan out of the series had an effect on the whole

third season. Apart from the rewrites to every script already in the planning stages, it also changed the dynamic of the show. "Zhaan was the stabilising influence on the series, in terms of her being the mother figure — albeit a really bizarre mother — and the soul," Kemper explains. "So we decided to have a season where all of a sudden it's as if all the kids go away to university, and there's no mother figure to give them guidance. It was a very dark season for them all, by design. There was a darkness, because there was nobody giving them moral guidance."

Above: Filming season three's 'Losing Time'.

There were other changes behind the scenes as well. Tony Winley, who had been line producer of the second season, moved up into the producer's chair, with Lesley Parker taking his old role. Winley's predecessor Sue Milliken remained a key consulting figure. New writers joined *Farscape*, including American genre veteran Carleton Eastlake and Australian writer Matt Ford, each bringing a new sensibility to the show. Other key personnel remained from the second season, including production designer Tim Ferrier and composer Guy Gross, both of whom signed on for a full year.

The series also gained a new title sequence, edited by post-production supervisor Deb Peart, complete with a new arrangement of the title music by Guy Gross, adapting Subvision's original. Kemper carefully sowed seeds of the dilemma that John Crichton would face throughout the year into the new voiceover. Additionally, each episode now received an onscreen title, with the whole year deriving its name from Ricky Manning's opening episode, 'Season of Death'. It was a year that would see not just Zhaan die, but D'Argo, Chiana, Crais — and even John Crichton himself... ■

THE EPISODES

" You have *got* to be kidding me."

– John Crichton

> **Regular cast:** Ben Browder (John Crichton), Claudia Black (Aeryn Sun), Anthony Simcoe (Ka D'Argo), Virginia Hey (Zotoh Zhaan), Gigi Edgley (Chiana), Paul Goddard (Stark), Wayne Pygram (Scorpius), Lani Tupu (Crais), Tim Mieville and team (Rygel: movement), Jonathan Hardy (Rygel: voice), Sean Masterson and team (Pilot: movement), Lani Tupu (Pilot: voice)

> **Written by:** Richard Manning
> **Directed by:** Ian Watson
>
> **Guest cast:** Matt Newton (Jothee), David Franklin (Lt Braca), Hugh Keays-Byrne (Grunchlk), Thomas Holesgrove (Diagnosan Tocot/Plonek), Aaron Catalan (Officer Kobrin)

Unaware of Crichton's predicament, tension is increasing amongst Moya's crew and Pilot's patience is running low as they orbit the ice planet, awaiting news of Crichton's surgery. Unable to speak following the operation to remove the chip from his brain, Crichton is horrified to discover that the neural clone of Scorpius is still trapped in his mind. Meanwhile, the real Scorpius is making plans for his escape with the extracted wormhole technology. Awaiting the arrival of his Command Carrier and fearing discovery, Scorpius makes an unwilling puppet of the treacherous Grunchlk in order to persuade Moya's crew that he has already left the planet. However, when Rygel discovers the incoherent Crichton and Tocot's unconscious body, he performs CPR on the Diagnosan and alerts his crewmates...

> **Harvey to Crichton**
>
> "Scorpius has beaten you. Aeryn Sun is dead. Your power of speech is gone. The only one you'll ever talk to again is me."

"I had to do an episode which started with Crichton brain-dead, Aeryn dead and Scorpius with what he wanted," director Ian Watson recalls. "The problem was to turn it around in forty-two minutes so that Crichton had what he wanted, and Aeryn was back from the dead!"

Although David Kemper jokes that he writes a fiendish cliffhanger for each season and leaves it to Ricky Manning to figure out how to resolve it, Kemper knew the mechanism by which Aeryn would be returned to life. However, as Ian Watson points out, "*Farscape* has killed so many people so many times who have then come back from the dead, it was a problem to bring Aeryn back believably."

"We knew that soon there was going to be the exit of another beloved regular character," series creator Rockne S. O'Bannon says, "and we thought it was a great opportunity to pay for the return of Aeryn with something real, that would help keep the series grounded. Yes, we bring Aeryn back, but we don't wave a magic wand, or have a big battle which is really difficult, and at the end everybody is huffing and puffing, but otherwise fine. We pay for Aeryn's return with a death, the sacrifice of another character who we really care for."

Claudia Black feels that Aeryn had a problem accepting what Zhaan had done for her. "When she actually comes out of the pod, she fires at the two soldiers who are threatening Zhaan and Stark, but she doesn't acknowledge what Zhaan's done. She looks at her and there's an ambiguous moment where she doesn't acknowledge her verbally at all, and just asks where the others are. She wants to avoid the emotion. She can't quite come to grips with Zhaan's spiritual world — I suggested it was much more appropriate for Aeryn to say that Zhaan 'did a Unity thing' rather than say she 'did Unity with me'."

The return to the ice planet caused practical problems on set. "A snowstorm is a hard thing to pull off, but we got it working," Ian Watson explains. "We experimented with different types of material to blow for snow, and settled on finely-chopped shopping bags, to produce a type of plastic-y stuff that's blown out under jets of air." "Imagine three days of having *that* blown in your face!" Ben Browder comments.

To film the scenes where Rygel administers CPR to the dying Tocot, Mat McCoy "was the most uncomfortable he's ever been," Tim Mieville believes, because "we had to get someone underneath the puppet to do that. Mat had to get his hand in at a really weird angle."

Above: *D'Argo and Stark assist a disoriented Crichton.*

Next page: Plonek, the Scarran.

Having the same actor playing Tocot the Diagnosan and Plonek the Scarran also caused one minor problem — getting Thomas Holesgrove to kill himself! "In the morning I was in the Tocot costume," Holesgrove recalls, "and at the end of the session we did the first shot of him getting zapped. Then in the afternoon I went into the Scarran suit and did the shots with the Scarran's hand. They had a stand-in as Tocot for the actual shot."

Returning to reprise his role from 'Die Me, Dichotomy' was Hugh Keays-Byrne as Grunchlk. "He's one of those legends of bad guy acting," Ian Watson enthuses. "I was quietly told by the producer not to have too much spurting blood in the scene where Scorpius makes him bite his finger off," he adds. "It can deny the show the correct time slot. We shot and cut two versions of it — the fairly tame version which is in the final edit, and another one where he actually holds his finger up in front of him, and it's just squirting blood gratuitously, like a *Monty Python* sketch!" ∎

SUNS AND LOVERS

Written by: Justin Monjo	Guest cast: Matt Newton (Jothee), Leanna Walsmann
Directed by: Andrew Prowse	(Borlik), Thomas Holesgrove (Moordil), Jessica Fallico
	(Alien Girl), David Lucas (Cryoman)

The crew has stopped at a space station to take on supplies and get some much needed rest and recuperation. D'Argo is buying union tattoos to mark his relationship with Chiana, just as, on board Moya, Rygel is discovering the Nebari's deception with Jothee. However, when a major storm hits, and the station and Moya are damaged, the crew realise that they must live up to their reputations. While Crichton and Aeryn discover that the damage to the station might not just be caused by a force of nature, D'Argo surveys the damage to Moya, and discovers an alien craft which he brings on board the Leviathan. Matters are made worse when Chiana spots the face of a panicked child, trapped in the lower levels of the station...

> ### Rygel to Crichton
>
> "I don't give a sisil's arse about a trapped girl."
>
> "And that's what makes you a great humanitarian, Buckwheat."

"Justin had read the book *The Perfect Storm*, and loved it," David Kemper recalls. "When it came to start working on his episode, he said he wanted to do a storm, because it's a great visual. It turned out to be one of those fun episodes to pull together, because it's early in the year, and you're not too worried about things. We wanted to get Crichton and Aeryn back on track."

"Without knocking it, this is a stock *Farscape* episode where you have really queer things going on," Andrew Prowse agrees. "But the emotional core of the story is D'Argo being betrayed. Anthony Simcoe did a great job with that. He gave D'Argo an extraordinary dignity through the discovery of his son's affair with Chiana. From the first scenes where he smells something, to the final poignant moments when he overhears the two lovers saying their goodbyes, it never feels mawkish and you willingly go with him. I also think that relationship between Jothee and Chiana really worked, being scary and fraught with danger. It was almost Romeo and Juliet-ish, with them in an environment that could have killed them, and I think the actors pulled it off really well."

ENCOUNTERS: KAMPEKS

A religious sect, that worships the god Kisma. They are noble warriors who believe that the traders on the space station are an affront to their doctrines, and prepare to instigate a cleansing apocalypse to restore the balance of the sacred space.

Gigi Edgley enjoyed shooting the betrayal scene with Simcoe and Matt Newton. "When you hit those really big, important scenes, you've got to almost tear them apart, dive into them, swim around for a bit and get yourself nice and wet, then get out and dry yourself off!" she enthuses. "You can't just dabble, 'in and out', because you never really feel that fulfilled after you finish the scene. Originally, the writers wanted Jothee to stick around a little bit longer," Edgley adds, "but Matt has had real success in Australia, and he's been kept busy elsewhere."

"The logistics of that episode were enormous," David Kemper recalls. "The space station was a lot of work, but it was a masterpiece," Andrew Prowse adds. "Production designer Tim Ferrier was very anxious to show off his wares, and it marked the beginning of the CG house, Animal Logic, really hitting their stride.

"The Moya skin set was very cool," Prowse continues. "It's the first time we've really been outside Moya and interacted with her. Tim did a great job with the set, but shooting on it was not simple. We shot most of it with a remote camera and a crane, looking down, to avoid having to do too much CG afterwards."

The tunnels also caused practical problems. "They were filmed with a

hand-held camera, by Danny Baterham," Prowse says. "There was a lot of water and rubbish on the floors, so just walking around took a lot of concentration." Not being able to move at great speed affected Claudia Black. "The hardest thing was playing the high urgency without being able to move quickly, which felt very awkward," she remembers.

David Kemper loves the repartee between Crichton and Aeryn. "Claudia did this great business in the tunnel where she and Ben are teasing each other," he recalls. At the time though, it puzzled the actors. "Neither Andrew, Ben nor I could understand why Aeryn offers herself to Crichton and he turns her down," Claudia Black says. "My immediate reaction was that he would say yes," reasons Ben Browder, "but essentially it becomes a bit of a power play. Aeryn wants to have her cake and eat it too, and pretend that things aren't as they are. He's hitting the ball back into her court and saying, 'You're going to have to admit you really like me, and *then* you can have me!'"

'Suns and Lovers' marked the first time that Thomas Holesgrove was heard as well as seen. "Being able to use my voice was terribly exciting," he recalls. "I used a very 'la-di-dah' British accent on set, but then the director asked me to dub it in an Eastern European accent." ■

Opposite page: Zhaan tends to Moordil.

Above: *Aeryn leads the children through the tunnels.*

SELF-INFLICTED WOUNDS
PART I: COULD'A, WOULD'A, SHOULD'A

Written by: David Kemper	**Introducing:** Tammy MacIntosh (Jool)
Directed by: Tony Tilse	**Guest cast:** Victoria Longley (Neeyala), Nicholas Hope (Kreetago), Dwayne Fernandez (Cresto), Kerith Atkinson (Shreena), Brian Carbee (Lastren)

While D'Argo is still reeling from the shock of discovering Chiana and Jothee's treachery, the crew head for a suitable planet on which to plant the ailing Zhaan. However, before they reach their destination, Pilot discovers a wormhole and Crichton excitedly insists that they investigate it. Before he can begin, another ship emerges, colliding and fusing with Moya. Both ships are trapped within the wall of the wormhole, between the passage and real space. Once again, the Leviathan is seriously injured, and while Crichton and the alien leader, Pathfinder Neeyala, try to understand what has happened, the other crewmembers, now including the disoriented Interion, Jool, are desperate to keep Moya strong enough to attempt to StarBurst. Unfortunately, the damage is too severe, and although they all realise that the ships will need to be separated, only one will survive intact...

> **Crichton to Harvey**
>
> "If he masters wormhole technology, what will he use it for?"
>
> "Faster delivery of pizzas."

"In February 1998, Rockne O'Bannon and I were coming up with more ideas for the show," David Kemper explains. "One I had was, 'A ship comes out of another dimension, but it hasn't fully resolved its form, and it comes flashing through our ship. We get merged with them — what the hell just happened?'"

'Self-Inflicted Wounds' went through numerous changes during pre-production, mainly as a result of Virginia Hey's departure. "Originally Zhaan survived," Kemper reveals, "but then the story had to become about giving one of your good characters a magnificent ending." Although

ENCOUNTERS: INTERIONS

From a peaceful star system, Interions value learning above all else and consider themselves intellectually superior to most other races. Although they share some genetic similarities with humans, there are some obvious differences: their cranial structure is decidedly non-human, their hair changes colour when angry or scared and they have a scream that can melt metal.

he feels it got diluted in the final version, Kemper also "wanted to explore how innocent people ended up dying because of their encounter with us. Neeyala's people weren't villains. They weren't trying to kill us. She could have wiped us out, but she didn't, and she died because of it. That's *Farscape*, and that's also the real world — I wanted to deal with the irony and capriciousness of death."

"Two-parters are always really tough, because they tend to be bigger stories with big emotional arcs," Tony Tilse explains. "David wrote a huge script, which came with its own logistical problems." One of these was the requirement for a large snake. "David was always very keen to have a wormhole beast; a scavenger that cleaned up all the refuse in the wormhole," Tilse says. "It was one of the few times we had a completely computer-generated monster. It's always interesting for the cast, with the director trying to describe what this creature will look like, because all we had were some drawings. The creature was still in development." To help the actors on set, the Creature Shop created a basic prop: "an open-mouthed thing with sharp fangs," Claudia Black recalls. "But in the end, it was one of the most incredible effects I have ever seen."

Having directed Victoria Longley before on another production, Tony

Above: Neeyala contemplates her next move.

Next page: Crichton tells Harvey to remove his father's tuxedo.

Tilse enjoyed the chance to work with her again. "We spent an afternoon discussing how these creatures spoke, with the lisp," he recalls. "We looked at the body language, and the way they walked — they had a lizardy feel to them."

Team Rygel had fun with the scene where the Hynerian joins Crichton in a tour round the wormhole. "It was cramped, sure," Tim Mieville says, "but when it's a very small set like that, we can get our controls right there, so we feel very much part of it. It was a full-on scene that ended up being quite violent."

Mieville is full of praise for Paul Goddard's performance opposite a rather sick Pilot. "Paul had a vomit gun about a foot away from his head," he recalls. "To be able to deliver those lines, knowing that he was about to get a face-full of intergalactic carrot chunks, was tremendous!"

The writers felt it was the right time for Crichton to be reminded of home. "Everyone jumped in with ideas for what it was going to be that Crichton saw from Earth," Kemper remembers: "*I Love Lucy*, *Mr Ed*, the Marx Brothers. Finally, I said that it had to be the Three Stooges. I wanted a specific clip where they're all together and Curly gets abused, because I knew that Scorpius was going to ask Crichton why it is always the innocent that bear the brunt for our dreams and ambitions." ■

SELF-INFLICTED WOUNDS
PART II: WAIT FOR THE WHEEL

Written by: David Kemper Directed by: Tony Tilse	Guest cast: Victoria Longley (Neeyala), Nicholas Hope (Kreetago), Dwayne Fernandez (Cresto), Kerith Atkinson (Shreena), Brian Carbee (Lastren)

Checking through the data that he and Rygel collected during their trip through the wormhole, Crichton discovers a transmission from Earth. But the rest of the crew have little time for this, as they are more concerned with their immediate situation. After Crichton's battle with the wormhole serpent, they find blood on the floor of Pilot's chamber. Zhaan identifies it as belonging to the aliens, leading them to the conclusion that there could be an invisible Pathfinder stalking the ship. The crew realise Neeyala clearly hasn't been completely honest with them, and they are being manipulated into abandoning Moya. Confronted, Neeyala finally admits that her subordinate Kreetago is sabotaging the Leviathan. As D'Argo and Chiana hunt Kreetago down, Neeyala's Phaztillon Generator reaches its optimization phase — there is only one arn left to save Moya and Pilot, and someone must make the ultimate sacrifice…

> **Crichton to Jool**
>
> "Look, Princess, I know that this trip to Kruegerland was not on your itinerary, but believe it or not, I know exactly how you feel."

"After a while of walking into pulsefire and getting out of impossible situations, you can start to believe in your own immortality," Ben Browder believes. "The death of Zhaan inherently changes the nature of the series, and reinforces the idea that death is real, even at this end of the universe. She's the first major character, who's been with us since the beginning, who we've lost in a permanent fashion. By that I mean she didn't disappear and come back three episodes later!"

Although Zhaan's death marked the highpoint of the emotional crescendo in the episode, other emotions were stirring, in part caused by the

ENCOUNTERS: PATHFINDERS

An intellectual species which travels through space in research vessels, and has acquired wormhole technology. Scientists who are sent on missions are given an extra incentive to succeed, as failure results in the execution of their families. Pathfinders' means of personal defence is through poisoned bristles, which they shoot from gill-like orifices on the sides of their heads.

arrival of Jool. "Jool was never going to be instantly likeable," Tony Tilse points out, while emphasising that this applied to the character, not the actress. "From the very beginning of our first scenes, Gigi and I had an open agreement to really go for it together," Tammy MacIntosh recalls. "We know how to push each other in a scene," Edgley agrees. "She's a method-based actor like me, so it's nice having another kid running round the set actually believing she's an alien as well!"

Claudia Black notes that "Aeryn is starting to get concerned about Crichton having seen the Three Stooges, because she now sees it's a possibility that he could get back to Earth, so the wheel starts again for her. I threw in the 'Yoda from Dagobah' line — I thought it was time for her to understand enough of the Earth references to get them wrong. She presumes when he's seen TV, it must be *Star Wars* again." Aeryn is also affected by Zhaan's increasing debilitation: "She's having to make decisions about Zhaan, because she feels the weight of Zhaan's illness the most, and it's really starting to take its toll."

Virginia Hey is grateful that Kemper wrote Zhaan such a good death scene. "It was heart-wrenching for me to complete my relationship with each of the main characters," she recalls. "It evoked the most intense emotion within me." Anthony Simcoe adds, "I think it was handled really sensitively, appro-

priately and definitively. We'd had so many 'fake' deaths that we wanted to appreciate the gravity of the moment." Gigi Edgley recalls the emotion of the moment spilling over. "All the truthful stuff was coming through," she says, "and we both started crying. There was blue and white make-up, then dark blue and light blue — we were like two little ice creams melting into one. They had to stop the scene!"

Tony Tilse wanted to go to a real drive-in cinema to shoot the final sequence, but unfortunately that wasn't possible. "The art department made me a little miniature screen that we ended up actually projecting onto," he recalls, "and then we inserted that over the main image." "The night before we shot the drive-in, we didn't have the clearances to use the Three Stooges clip you see in the scene," David Kemper adds. "We'd had months to sort it out, but we didn't get the clearances until three minutes before we shot it!"

Tilse enjoyed all the challenges of visualising the episode. "When D'Argo plans to catch the invisible guy, there was no CG involved," he recalls. "We put dry ice on the ground, then put a little puffer on a roller-skate tied to a string, which we pulled underneath the fog and puffed the dry ice up. It gave the illusion of someone invisible moving through the fog. And those laser beams were all real, too." ∎

Opposite page: Zhaan comforts D'Argo.

Above: Crichton and Harvey at the drive-in.

Written by: Steve Worland **Directed by:** Peter Andrikidis	**Guest cast:** Lucy Bell (Nurse Kelsa), Basia A'hern (Cyntrina), Marshall Napier (General Grynes), Dan Spielman (Sub-Officer Dacon), Terry Serio (Colonel Lennok), Alan Cinis (Officer Tarn)

While Chiana and Rygel mourn the loss of Zhaan and help Pilot repair Moya, the rest of the crew visit a peace memorial at a monastery on the verdant planet of Jocacea. As Aeryn and Jool bicker about Peacekeeper propaganda, Crichton shows D'Argo how to use a special mask to view the historic events of 500 cycles earlier: a group of nurses, aided by a small Peacekeeper unit, negotiated a surrender to the vastly superior Venek horde, and were saved from massacre. When Crichton persuades a grieving Stark that Zhaan would want him to share the moment of peace, he puts the mask on, but it reacts with his energy, opening a portal in time. Crichton and his party are somehow sucked through, and find themselves trapped in the past as the monastery comes under its final attack from the Venek horde...

Aeryn to Crichton

"If we did change things, it is possible that we could improve the future."

"With our record, do you think that's gonna happen?"

"We're not consciously trying to be different from other shows," David Kemper maintains. "We just want the audience to find something new." It's an approach that applies when it comes to dealing with a staple of TV science fiction, from *Doctor Who* to *Star Trek*: time travel. "Everyone expected us to put history right, because they grew up watching *Star Trek*," Kemper explains. "We would have gone back to the memorial at the end and read the history books, and seen that everything went back to normal. There might even be a mention of a Luxan who came and went like a magical phoenix. But that's not the *Farscape* way."

Peter Andrikidis, who was returning to the show as director nearly two years after helming season one's 'The Flax', loved the combination of styles within the episode. "It had a really good sense of humour to it, with what was happening to D'Argo and Stark," he points out, "with a balance

ENCOUNTERS: VENEKS

A race of leonine warriors. When they march as a horde, they are supposed to drive fear into the bravest of hearts. When entering into battle they achieve a level of ferocity termed 'blood lust', which remains in them until they satisfy their need for death.

of big dramatic moments and high comedy. Then it had that very black conclusion, which reminds me of *Back to the Future*, without the uplifting end. Our hero has actually affected the past, but it ends in a lot of deaths."

Ben Browder notes that "there is a darkness about the beginning of season three, in contrast to the start of our other seasons. It affects John in the same way that it affects the audience. The jokes become a little edgier and things become a little harder."

"I love sieges on film," Anthony Simcoe says, "and I also liked that episode because of the relationship D'Argo has with Cyntrina. It's the introduction of the third phase of D'Argo, as he makes some really mature decisions."

Although Steve Worland wrote the first draft of the episode, it fell to David Kemper and Justin Monjo to complete it. "Steve had his own series to work on," Kemper recalls, "so we redid the script. We knew we had the bones of a really great show. We had great drama and we had a twist ending that no one was going to expect. It was serious, it was funny, and it had very poignant moments. It turned into one of my favourite episodes of the year."

The comic moments allowed Anthony Simcoe and Tammy MacIntosh to shine. "David wrote this really beautiful comedy for Jool," MacIntosh says.

Above: Crichton tries to persuade Aeryn to follow his plan.

Next page: Nurse Kelsa holds Crichton at gunpoint.

"That was where I thought I had really found the character. When I had to drink the piss, I made it seem like it made me drunk. I was feeling really silly and stupid that day. There was no reference to that in the script, but I thought that it would be fun."

MacIntosh risked the wrath of the make-up department when she rolled in the mud. "Under no circumstances was that six thousand dollar wig to be put through the mud," she recalls, "because it would take at least ten hours to wash it, and re-tong every one of those little curls." So MacIntosh sent her make-up artist away from the set briefly. "I said to Peter, 'Quickly, quickly, let's do it!' So we shoot the scene, then Anna walks back in the door, and her face is white. Her jaw is on the floor and I'm rolling in the mud, loving it. The wig is absolutely trashed. It is brown, the curls have dropped out and it is just a dead, muddy wig. Anna didn't talk to me again for about three weeks!"

Claudia Black thinks '...Different Destinations' is a valuable reminder to viewers that their heroes are fallible. "That's an important journey for the audience," she says. "They see their heroes failing, but growing and learning from their experiences and mistakes." ∎

EAT ME

Written by: Matt Ford	Guest cast: Shane Briant (Kaarvok),
Directed by: Ian Watson	Lisa Griffiths (Belima)

eparated from Moya and running out of oxygen, Crichton, D'Argo, Chiana and Jool think they have reached safety when they spot a Leviathan. Then they see a Peacekeeper control collar and realise it is not Moya, but they are out of options so Crichton sets course for the ship despite the others' reservations. Upon landing, they try to make sense of the decay that permeates the ship, but quickly come under attack from a strange creature. Wanting to get away as quickly as possible, Crichton and D'Argo head off to find the parts they need to repair their damaged transport pod, while Chiana and Jool remain in the maintenance bay. Crichton realises that they will need the Pilot's help and searches for his den, and Chiana abandons Jool to warn the others that the pod is being affected by the decay. But when Crichton finds the unfortunate Pilot, he is a gibbering wreck, and begs the human to kill him…

Aeryn to Rygel

" If you try anything while I'm gone, whatever you have in the place of mivonks and wherever they are, they will be gone when I get back."

"I *loved* the script when I read it," director Ian Watson enthuses. "The thing I liked about season two was that it had a lot of eccentric one-off episodes, and 'Eat Me' was reminiscent of those. It's a fantastic, hard, tough, dark episode written by a new writer, who himself is an eccentric individual."

David Kemper recalls that Matt Ford, who combines fronting rock band MGF with his writing work, asked to do an episode about cannibalism. "We knew we wanted to split Crichton, but we didn't know how," he explains. "We came up with the idea of a villain trapped on a ship who twinned people, so that he would have a bigger food source. But if you twinned people enough times, their cellular structure degenerated to a degree that the person was no longer viable. It was our second dark episode in a row."

ENCOUNTERS: XARAI

Kaarvok's affectionate nickname for his former Peacekeeper captors, whom he has repeatedly twinned, draining their brains of the essence that he requires to survive. With each successive twinning, the Xarai have increasingly begun to look like mutants, and have resorted to eating their Leviathan prison to stay alive.

True to the overall theme of the 'Season of Death', 'Eat Me' sees a number of the crew killed. "Kaarvok drives a spike through D'Argo's head, and the audience is wondering what happened!" Kemper says. "They must be pretty sure that we haven't killed off a second lead character two weeks after Zhaan… So we revealed the truth to everyone except Crichton, who doesn't know until the end."

"The good thing about this episode is that it's a horror show," Watson maintains. "All the characters are pushed to their extremes. They all have to be taken to the point of really believing that they are going to die on this ship — this mouldy, rotten carcass of a Leviathan is where they will finally die."

Gigi Edgley revelled in the challenges posed to Chiana in this episode. "Both Chiana and Gigi had an awesome time experimenting," she recalls. "It was the first really juicy invitation to let Chiana come out and play. I am a hopeless romantic for dark scripts that challenge the character to explore a multitude of boundaries."

Playing the scene where Jool creeps out of the pod on her own spooked Tammy MacIntosh so much that "the sound guy said that I was so frightened that he couldn't hear my footsteps — all he could hear was my heartbeat! I really enjoyed that fear factor, and revealing the lack of hope — the despair that

Jool felt inside, rather than just having this brash, cover-up attitude all the time."

Simcoe was bodily dragged around the corridors of the other Leviathan, Rovhu. "I still tease Ian Watson about that," Simcoe says. "We got to the set, and of course you can't drag D'Argo around, not because I am big and heavy, but because of the practical problems of the prosthetics. I had to use my stomach and my neck muscles to lift my head slightly off the floor all the time. It was outrageously difficult and really tiring. I said to Ian, 'You didn't really think this through, did you?', and he called me obstructionist! The cheek!"

Sean Masterson and the Pilot team had a chance to experiment with Rovhu's Pilot. "I worked with Mario Halouvas inside the body to make the movements a lot more violent than our Pilot's movements," Masterson explains. "Generally Pilot rolls around at his console in a nice gentle way, and there's never anything staccato, abrupt or sharp. This Pilot had been tortured so much that it was actually changing his characteristics."

"You've got an exceptional set of circumstances in 'Eat Me'," Ben Browder points out. "Crichton is in a horror film, and he knows he's in a horror film. But he can't figure out how to get out of it, and it's getting worse and worse. Up to that episode, I think he was coping alright. But after that, well..." ■

Opposite page: *Kaarvok taunts D'Argo.*

Above: *Chiana faces off against the Xarai.*

THANKS FOR SHARING

Written by: Clayvon C. Harris	Guest cast: Rebecca Gibney (Sarova), Robert Brunning
Directed by: Ian Barry	(Pralanoth), Sandy Winton (Tolven), Linda Cropper (Xhalax Sun), Julianne Newbould (Felor), Hunter Perske (Bloy)

Crais lies critically ill and Talyn severely wounded as the two Crichtons struggle to come to terms with each other's existence. Moya is transfusing Talyn to keep him alive, but the gunship's only hope is that D'Argo, Chiana and Rygel will be able to acquire some Chromextin from the locals on Kanvia. While D'Argo and Rygel are negotiating purchase of the drug, Chiana receives some unwanted attention. D'Argo steps in to defend her and they unwittingly create a political situation that jeopardises the transaction. While Rygel attempts to talk his way into a solution, Crais recovers consciousness. He explains that a Peacekeeper Retrieval Squad has been sent after Talyn, injuring them both in its last attempt at capture. When he is left alone with Aeryn, Crais reveals his other piece of news — the Retrieval Squad is headed by none other than Senior Officer Xhalax Sun: Aeryn's mother...

> **Crichton to Stark**
>
> "Hey, Astro – work now, freak later."
>
> "Yes, that's fair... how much later?"

"'Thanks for Sharing' was a transitional episode from this dark, unrelenting rollercoaster to the middle portion of the year, which dealt with the two Crichtons," David Kemper explains. "It was a difficult episode to do on many levels, and Ricky Manning stepped in and guided the rewrite. We had to set up that Aeryn's mother was chasing her, which in turn set up 'Relativity' and 'The Choice'. We had to introduce the Colartas, who would feature in 'Relativity'. And we had to make it an episode in its own right."

Coming on board was new director Ian Barry. "I'd worked with prosthetics and normal visual effects before," he says, "but I'd never worked with puppets. I found it astonishing to watch Rygel being operated by ten people!"

Rygel and Pilot weren't the only puppets in this episode, as the puppetry team took responsibility for the truth-seeking Strannat. "There were various different versions so we could play around on set and see which one looked best for the shot," Sean Masterson reveals. "Some of the best

ENCOUNTERS: STRANNATS

Amphibious squid-like creatures, which can sense brainwave patterns and are extremely sensitive to cognitive dissonance. Used by the Kanvians as a lie detector, they are trained to kill immediately if they sense a lie being told.

shots were actually done just yanking fishwire in the water."

"Sometimes simple is best," Tim Mieville agrees. "It's one of those creatures that is so repulsive, you only have to half convince people that it's there. People move away from it instinctively. At the end when it was on Crichton's face and it's tracking his forehead to detect the lies, we only had to do a tiny bit of movement, and it was just so creepy."

Crais and Talyn had been reintroduced in 'Eat Me'. "We needed Crais back because half the crew had to fly away on Talyn," Kemper points out. "We also had to set the possibility up in the audience's mind, and therefore in Crichton's mind, that Crais and Aeryn had something going on. There's always been a good chemistry between Claudia and Lani, so we knew that would work." Claudia Black was delighted at the initial scene between Aeryn and Crais. "That comes quite a way into the season," she notes. "He's the last person amongst our regular characters to find out that she's actually alive." "I chose to underplay that, as though I had seen her but hadn't 'really' seen her," Lani Tupu recalls. "Sometimes things work a lot better underplayed, rather than going over the top — though Crais is not one to go over the top anyway."

Black also welcomed the casting of Aeryn's mother and younger self. "I've got baby photos where I look very similar to that girl, and I think Linda

Above: Chiana receives unwanted attention from Tolven and Bloy.

Next page: Crichton watches the Strannat attack Tolven.

Cropper is quite similar to me as well. In the flashbacks, I made the choice to nod when Xhalax asked if I was listening. It was nice synchronicity to bring the two Aeryns together."

Ben Browder's overwhelming memory of the episode is of trying to recall which T-shirt he was meant to be wearing. "For some reason, trying to track that through turned into something akin to calculus," he jokes. "We had lots of debates as to who was going to get what T-shirt, and then had to backtrack through the script because they swap clothes during the story. And then of course they were impersonating each other in that episode as well!"

The climactic transformation scene, revealing the Colarta, mixed CG and prosthetics. "We made the transition more as a series of shock cuts," Ian Barry observes. "We had to shoot that in fragments, and it took about three days!" Tim Mieville elaborates: "The Creature Shop made some great heads with the chin going two feet in one direction, and we had to move those really violently."

"We call that a 'meat and potatoes' episode," Kemper concludes. "We were stretched to the max logistically, because we had to do a lot of the show off Moya while those sets were being repainted after 'Eat Me', but it was a good story." ■

Written by: Ben Browder **Directed by:** Tony Tilse	**Regular cast only**

Separated from Moya, Crichton's temper is fraying as he finds himself stranded on Talyn with half the crew. His anger is further fuelled when he starts to believe that Crais is playing deliberate mindgames, sending DRDs in to plague him, and stealing his gun, Wynonna. Crichton confronts Crais and the two headstrong men erupt into an argument, oblivious to the impending danger outside the ship. When Stark and Rygel return from a recon mission, they find that Talyn (with Crichton, Aeryn and Crais on board) has been swallowed by a Budong. While the Banik and the Hynerian play cat and mouse to avoid the same fate, Crichton and Aeryn use a torpedo to anchor Talyn to the interior of the Budong, preventing them from being swept into the huge creature's fiery stomach. While they catch their breath, Crichton searches Crais's quarters. To his horror, he discovers a vidchip showing Aeryn and Crais 'recreating'…

> **Crichton to Aeryn**
>
> "See that star? The bright one. Wherever we go, there's always one bright star. It always becomes the centre of my chart… my point of reference. My guide. I've named it Aeryn."

Ben Browder and David Kemper were in the middle of a British SCI FI Channel Internet chat in September 2000, when the executive producer suddenly announced that the series star would be penning an episode for the third season. "Ben sent me a private e-mail asking what I was doing! Well, I'd read a couple of the feature film scripts Ben had written, and I knew he had a writer's instinct inside," Kemper explains. "We gave him endless amounts of notes and rewrites on 'Green Eyed Monster', but he just kept going. He wrote every word of that script himself."

"I find that when I'm writing, I play the scene in my head," Browder comments. "But I really noticed that when I walked on set, it was like I was hearing the lines for the first time. I would find myself in the middle of rehearsal drying up a lot more than anyone else, and I wrote the damn thing!"

Executive consultant Carleton Eastlake is full of praise for the episode. "It was one of my favourite scripts of the year," he says. "I thought it was just wonderful the way it handled this romantic triangle, and the subconscious tensions that are maybe being acted out through Talyn, together with a very fresh and very tight action story."

"Part of the drama of 'Green Eyed Monster' is that Aeryn can't understand why Crichton is acting like such a complete doofus," Claudia

Black points out. "The whole episode is structured ambiguously, so that at the beginning you're not sure where your sympathy should lie. Is Crichton being jealous or is there a conspiracy?"

Tony Tilse approached the story as "a good old-fashioned submarine drama. These people are trapped in this ship, and it's claustrophobic. There was a hothouse of emotion going on." The scenes with Stark and Rygel acted as comic relief, and Tilse used them to maintain the emotional balance. "But that comic element can be destructive to the overall mood," he warns. "It can be annoying if all you want to do is get back to the main story, so it was really important that we didn't spend too much time there."

In his script, Browder referred to 'Tilsie-vision' when describing the distinctive look that he wanted for Talyn's point of view. "I had to come up with a practical way of doing that, so I resorted to my old favourite method," Tilse explains. "We use handy little video cameras and then treat them in post-production. We ramped up the colour to give it a lovely kind of floating energy, and you can then warp the edges of the image. I think Martin Connor, the editor, had recently seen *2001: A Space Odyssey* again, and he put a lot of those ideas in there." The live Budong

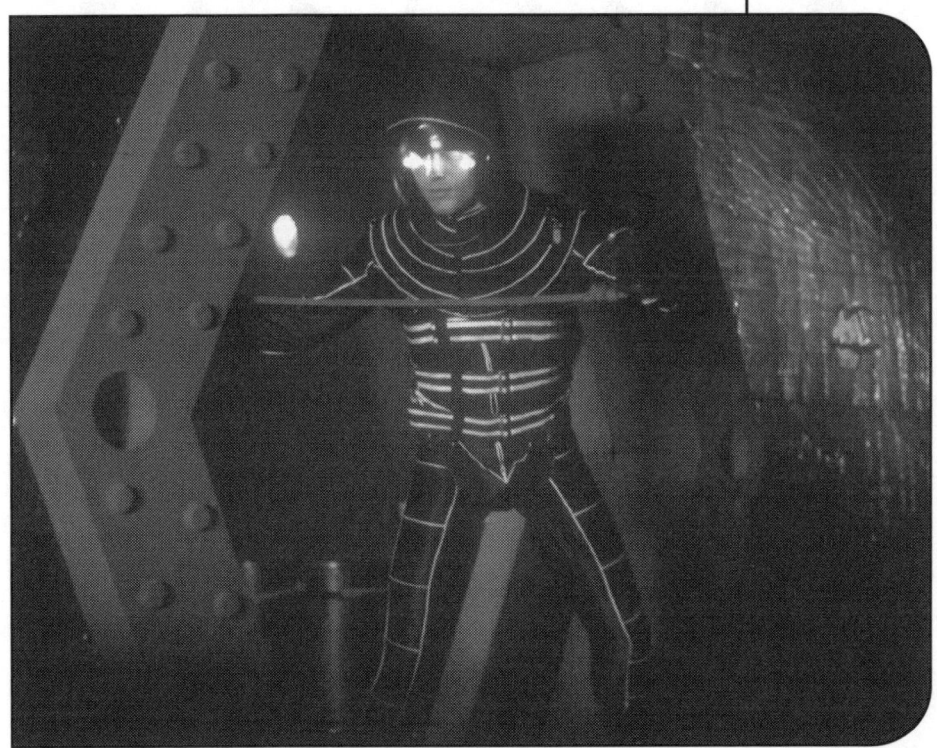

was created by Animal Logic. "We couldn't see the whole of it, because even the CG department couldn't cope with the full length of a Budong," Tilse jokes.

Opposite page: Crais is tormented by Talyn.

Before 'Green Eyed Monster' was filmed, the Talyn bridge set was rebuilt. "It was a functionality issue," David Kemper explains. "When you've been shooting in there for a year, there are things that work and things that suck. We didn't redesign the ship, just the way the set was constructed — where the camera team could turn around or what you could do with certain sections."

Above: Crichton exits Talyn to set the charges.

By this stage, the producers knew Talyn's destiny in 'Into the Lion's Den'. "We began the process of laying that in place," Kemper says. "We had Talyn acting on his own, trying to hurt Crichton and make his 'dad' get the girl."

Claudia Black recalls a "nice little plug for my film career. When Aeryn's trying to shoot the torpedo, she says 'still nothing — pitch black'. But I wasn't giving myself a shameless plug — Ben was!"

"We still took a pretty liberal approach to the text," Browder concludes. "But at least we had the writer on the set with us each day!" ■

LOSING TIME

Written by: Justin Monjo Directed by: Catherine Millar	Guest cast: David Franklin (Lt Braca), Jo Kerrigan (Linfer), Danny Adcock (Co-Kura Strappa), Ian Bliss (PK Scientist Drillic), Tux Akindoyeni (PK Pilot Rinon)

Plagued by nightmares about his quest for the secrets of wormhole technology, Scorpius is woken to be told that his scientific team has succeeded in creating a wormhole. Encouraged by their results, the team agree it is time to commence piloted flights. Moya detects possible wormhole activity and while Crichton, D'Argo, Chiana and Jool are arguing about investigating further, an entity invades the ship and assaults Crichton. Although he levitates, and bleeds profusely, all signs of injury and the spilt blood disappear before he can show them to his shipmates. The others accordingly treat his story with scepticism, until they all simultaneously experience time loss. Trying to obtain answers from Pilot, the crew discover him unconscious — until he comes back to life, declaring "judgment starts now..."

Crichton

"I am bleeding and I have no wounds. So I'm either Saint John of the Uncharted Territories or there's something very, very wrong with me."

The initial inspiration for 'Losing Time' came from a bizarre incident at Ben Browder's audition for Rockne S. O'Bannon and David Kemper many years earlier, when the actor had spontaneously started bleeding. "Justin had always said that he wanted to do something with that image," David Kemper recalls. "So he came up with the idea of a being coming into the ship, then Crichton suddenly has blood running down his head, and doesn't remember it happening. This was also the first solo Moya episode after the split. We knew we had some funny Moya stories coming up, so we wanted a serious one, which set our people against each other. It had to be a character piece, which Justin is great at. It all leaps off the screen in a funny way, yet there's a drama being played out."

The episode saw Gigi Edgley give what Ben Browder describes as "a really brave, fantastic performance. She was so convincing as the possessed

ENCOUNTERS: ENERGY RIDER

An ethereal creature, composed of energy, not matter. It infects and takes over matter-based lifeforms, feeding on their life-force for a short time before moving on to the next 'host'. Whilst possessed by a rider, the infected being is physically much more powerful, and its own individual personality is suppressed — the rider 'speaks' through the physical vessel.

Chiana." Edgley herself explains, "I thought the energy rider would be a lot more evil if she initially tasted as sweet as the sweetest of temptation's juice that dribbles from Adam's apple! I workshopped a few different forms of possession," she continues. "I tried to imagine what this rider would sound like. It seemed to be androgynous, flighty, cheeky and spontaneous. It had travelled through many worlds and tasted many spirits. I figured that it had to be inspired by the moment, to use whatever technique it knew to manipulate the person it was confronted by at the time. The first person the rider had to convince was Crichton, so I tried to conjure the most inviting creature that Crichton could imagine, yet still remain truthful to the fact that it was an alien species."

"That was the start of Chiana having an ability to see the future," Kemper adds. "Justin wondered what would happen if after she's been possessed, something changes in her. We didn't want to give her a 'super power' that she could use any time, but something that could grow, and be different and interesting."

Pilot's possession posed a challenge for the puppetry team. "Mario Halouvas pushed physically within the body to try and do something new, and he came up with the goods," Sean Masterson comments. "We extended what we were doing in 'Eat Me', and really got into it!"

Above: Crichton attacks Scorpius in the hybrid's nightmare.

Next page: The energy rider possesses Chiana.

ning pe.

Ben Browder most clearly remembers "the death of DRD Pike. We named him on the set — Pike was an obscure reference from those of us who love the original series of *Star Trek*. But after you've named the character, and he doesn't get out of the StarBurst chamber, that's a tragic moment. How does it happen that these mechanical objects, that just blink once for yes and twice for no, are imbued with a character that you actually care about? I found it really sad when little DRD Pike died."

While 'Losing Time' was in pre-production, the writing team was also working ahead on 'Incubator'. "We knew that we wanted to get to the Command Carrier at the end of the season," David Kemper explains, "so we took the opportunity to put in a 'B' story to set up 'Incubator', which in turn set up the end of the year. We introduced some characters who would play through the whole year, and gave it some continuity."

Co-Kura Strappa was played by Danny Adcock, who had impressed the production team as Traltixx in season two's 'Crackers Don't Matter'. "He's someone who can play comedy and drama, and he knows how to move and act under prosthetics," praises Kemper. "You can use him over and over under prosthetic, and he's not afraid. He's our male Francesca Buller!" ■

Written by: Rockne S. O'Bannon Directed by: Peter Andrikidis	Guest cast: Linda Cropper (Xhalax Sun), Thomas Holesgrove (Vek), Dominique Sweeney (Thek and Kek)

While Crichton and Aeryn are rediscovering their love for each other, Talyn is powered down and recuperating on a jungle planet. However, their downtime is abruptly curtailed when Talyn detects the arrival of the Peacekeeper Retrieval Squad, headed by Aeryn's mother. Xhalax Sun is accompanied by two Colarta mercenaries, Thek and Vek, who proceed to follow Talyn's trail. Unable to leave, or locate the exact position of the Peacekeeper craft, Crichton, Aeryn and Crais have no choice but to go out onto the planet's inhospitable surface to draw their hunters away, and give Talyn the time he needs to recover. Alerted by the shots that Crichton fires, Xhalax takes the bait and heads away from Talyn — as Stark and Rygel discover that the planet's vegetation is threatening to overrun the ship...

> ### Stark to Rygel
>
> "Friend or foe, friend or foe?"
>
> "Of course it's a foe! We have no friends."

"Claudia and I had a great rapport, as people and as actors," guest star Linda Cropper says. "I think we just locked very instinctively into each other's dynamic in a way, and we didn't need to do a lot of talking through the mother/daughter relationship."

"I was delighted that we ended up having more than one episode together," Claudia Black adds. "I didn't think that they would weave Aeryn's mother back into the storyline that much. It's also a very accessible storyline, because if she's alive, then it's possible we can encounter her on numerous occasions." David Kemper comments, "We've been waiting a long time to bring Aeryn together with her mother. It was good for the third season to flesh Aeryn out in that way, and bring her some closure."

"It was mostly a very unsentimental episode," Rockne S. O'Bannon points out. "So therefore the scenes that *are* sentimental, or have heart and emotion, are just that bit more potent. Early on, when Xhalax is

ENCOUNTERS: COLARTAS

Colartas are enslaved mercenaries with multiple hearts, whose highly developed senses make them perfect trackers. They have an acute sense of smell, exceptional hearing and can detect the heat signatures of hidden quarry. They are capable of shape-shifting, assuming the appearance and voice of other beings. They must successfully complete nine missions to earn their freedom from the Peacekeepers.

unconscious, and Aeryn touches her face — that's such a tender moment." As well as the dynamic between Aeryn and Xhalax Sun, "'Relativity' is also about Crichton and Crais," O'Bannon continues. "Crais yet again shows himself to have betrayed everybody for his own purposes."

"It's always hard to see Crais as a baddie," director Peter Andrikidis admits. "Even with the villains, David tries to make sure that it's not black and white. I think they developed that character really well."

The biggest problem for every department was the jungle set. "I still hate the vines," Andrikidis says. "They ended up being made of rope, because of big safety issues. The floors were very slippery. Claudia fell over in the big chase scene, and everyone was just slipping everywhere."

"I could see maybe a metre in front of me on the ground," Thomas Holesgrove recalls. "There were a lot of very low hanging vines and things to bang your head on!" Ben Browder is more blunt. "That set was a real pain in the butt, because of the wood chips on the floor," he says. "It was very tricky to film in, and Peter did a magnificent job shooting there. It's a difficult episode, because you're dealing with a space where it's very difficult to define any sense of geography. When you shoot on a set like that,

there's a danger that you can lose the threads of the story. That's not taking anything away from the art department — creating a jungle on the floor of a warehouse is very difficult to do. It's beautiful work, and in fast turnaround television, a jungle is a very difficult thing to 'sell' to the viewer, so I think Peter and everyone involved did a very good job."

"We wanted to do *Predator* in the jungle set with the Colartas," explains Kemper. "But the reality of film-making is that it's hard to make these gigantic creatures run and jump, because the guys have got a million dollars' worth of electronics on their head! So instead of making the Colartas fast and sleek, we made them more like grizzly bears that can crash through the undergrowth, and have special tracking and weaponry skills."

Team Rygel enjoyed the Hynerian Dominar's role in 'Relativity'. "We had a fair bit of action, and Rygel had to carry it through — no one else could do it," Tim Mieville says. "Because Rygel has short arms, it's very hard to convey if he's hacking anything, so we decided he'd saw his way through, which was easier for us to do. Stark ended up doing most of the work, but it didn't matter, as that was typical of Rygel. We're lucky that we have a character who has a regal personality — it helps us justify why he's not doing something!" ■

Opposite page: Aeryn *assesses her mother's injury.*

Above: *The Colarta trackers, Vek and Kek.*

Written by: Richard Manning	Guest cast: David Franklin (Lt Braca), Amy Salas (Tauza),
Directed by: Ian Watson	Evan Sheaves (Child Scorpius), Stephanie Jacobsen (Nurse Froy), Paul Shedlowich (Plint), Jo Kerrigan (Linfer), Danny Adcock (Co-Kura Strappa), Thomas Holesgrove (Wolesh), Sam Healy (Rylani Jeema Dellos), Nicholas Bishop (Ghebb Dellos), William Zappa (Captain Molayne)

Although Scorpius's team of scientists is able to sustain a wormhole, anyone who tries to go through it is liquefied. When Co-Kura Strappa discovers that part of the wormhole technology is encrypted, his crew are thrown into a heated scientific debate. Linfer is so convinced that she can solve the phase variance, she volunteers to pilot the next test flight. In desperation, Scorpius inserts the neural chip into his own head, and summons a Crichton neural clone. In order to make the clone understand the Scarran threat, Scorpius decides to reveal his origins. Meanwhile, Linfer's test flight is successful, and she arrives near Moya. Fearing a trap, none of the crew wish to let her come on board, but for once Pilot and Moya override their decsion, and allow Linfer to dock. Crichton is amazed to hear that she comes bearing "the secret to wormhole travel"…

> **Crichton to D'Argo**
>
> "Do you ever think we've been on this boat way too long?"
>
> "Constantly."

On the 'Ideas' pin-board in the writers' room at Homebush Bay are a number of file cards. Some simply bear one word, others might have a sentence, or a description of an image. Some of them have initials at the bottom, indicating whose idea it was. Since the start of the second season, one has sat there, bearing the initials RM: 'A Day in the Life of Scorpius'.

"Everyone has their own pet project, and this was Ricky's," David Kemper explains. "It would be a Scorpius episode — we'd follow him around, not as if he's a guest star, but as his episode. It didn't fit in the second year, but this year it did. We had lost sight of Scorpius for a while, because we knew we were going to get to him at the end of the year. We wanted our people to get away from him, to have other adventures. Ricky suggested showing what Scorpius was doing with wormholes. The audience and Crichton needed to know how far along he had got, so Crichton could later make his decision to go to the Command Carrier."

"Ricky wrote it in a way that prescribed Scorpius as the hero of the story," director Ian Watson adds. "If we didn't know better, this is the story of a tortured, parentless young man. He's raised under adverse conditions, where he realises that the people who protect him are actually his captors.

He breaks out, and tries to find his own identity."

"You don't normally get this with a villain," Rockne S. O'Bannon comments. "It opens a door to his psyche. Usually the villains just address you with their own villainous agenda, as opposed to you really getting a sense of what they're thinking beyond that."

Although Crichton is not actually present, Kemper believes that Scorpius is telling his version of the astronaut the truth, at least as he sees it. "He isn't so weak that he needs justification from the clone," he points out. "There may be another layer beneath it, but I don't think he's actively chosen to lie to the clone, because it would not serve his purposes."

"I was vaguely resetting the clone to the Crichton at the time the chip was removed in 'Die Me, Dichotomy'," Ben Browder says. "His attitude towards Scorpius is all tinged by the fact that, to him, Aeryn has just died. Scorpy was knocking on the wrong door there!"

Wayne Pygram worked extensively with Evan Sheaves to ensure a continuity of Scorpius's mannerisms. "We had to believe that this boy was the young Scorpius," Watson points out. "We revoiced the boy with Wayne doing a younger version of himself, but it's a fantastic performance from Evan."

Above: A younger
Scorpius in pain.

Next page: Scorpius
and Captain Molayne.

Watson deliberately gave 'Incubator' an unusual visual style. "The challenge was to do an episode which didn't feature the usual characters as much, and make it visually interesting," he explains. "I didn't dolly or put the camera on wheels once — the camera is either fixed, or it pans. I wanted it to be much more static and create a sense of snapshots from Scorpius's past."

The rape that led to Scorpius's conception caused some concern. "There was a lot of discussion about that scene," Watson recalls. "We were concerned about the level of implied violence. I told Sam Healey that I wanted the emotional intensity of what was happening to read on her face, and that when the scene was finished, I wanted every male in the room to feel guilty."

"We knew that Ian had a handle on the material from way back," Kemper says, "and all the pieces looked really good going in. There was a special feel when it was done — it turned into one of our really startling episodes, but it was still *Farscape*." ■

Written by: Matt Ford	**Guest cast:** Sierjna (Susan Lyons), Mu-Quillus (Mark
Directed by: Ian Barry	Mitchell), Xhalax Sun (Linda Cropper)

Still distrustful of Crais, Crichton accuses him of cutting a deal with the Peacekeepers. Once again their arguments distract them, and they fail to notice Talyn altering course to fly on a direct collision course with a star. Despite feeling irrationally compelled to fly straight into the sun, after desperate persuasion from Crais and the rest of the crew, Talyn manages to enter orbit instead. When they discover that drexim fluid is seeping through the ship's corridors, the crew begin to find they are having difficulty controlling their basic instincts, and become disoriented and unable to function as a group. Then, when a strange woman materialises in front of Stark seeking Talyn's Pilot, and another alien appears on the bridge, it becomes clear that the crew have more problems than simple solar radiation to deal with…

Crichton to Stark

" Aeryn is my Zhaan, she's my Zhaan in every way. I love her and I would die for her..."

"There's a method to our madness," David Kemper points out. "Not much on our show is done haphazardly. I knew that the Talyn side of the split Crichton story was laid out linearly: we had an overall storyline written, and we had to follow it. I wanted to make the Moya crew's side much more one-by-one episodic television. 'Meltdown' was the one episode for the Talyn crew when we could step away from it being all about Mom, and Crichton and Aeryn. The villain was a guy who stood alone. He came in and left in one episode, yet it still played to advance the Crichton and Aeryn love story, under another guise."

Ian Barry returned for his second episode in the director's chair, and found he enjoyed the experience even more. "'Meltdown' went through an extraordinarily eleventh hour process, but it all came together because they've got a very strong team on the show," he says. "It set up a straightforward premise, then it had a lot of character drive. 'Thanks for Sharing' had a very intricate, convoluted plot, and sometimes the intensity of a story can

ENCOUNTERS: MU-QUILLUS

An alien hybrid with lava-like skin, able to switch between a matter and an energy state, who exists within the corona of a star. He is under contract with the Prahtikrah, a race of ancient ship-builders who feel that their industry is threatened by Leviathans. His brief is to lure Leviathans to their death within the star — a task he enjoys.

make the characters slaves to the plot, but 'Meltdown' gave some room to play, particularly for Ben and Claudia."

"I'm glad it was Claudia I was doing that episode with," Ben Browder admits. "We have a remarkable working relationship, in that we're really good friends, and the boundaries of our working relationship are very clear and well drawn. We don't get into that uneasy space that you often get into working with someone that closely. It's proof that we work really well together that we could do that episode without getting stressed about it."

Black agrees: "It was very difficult to shoot, but it was funny, because Ben and I spent all our time on set kissing! Normally in rehearsals we'll mark the point to 'insert kiss here' on the day, and sometimes the crew will ask us in a very perfunctory way to get into kissing positions. On this episode, we had to do it in rehearsals, and the crew were standing around going, 'Oh God, they're going to kiss again. Let's go and make a cup of coffee!'"

The pacing of the episode was adapted in the editing room. "Ben, Claudia and Ian Barry went pretty hard at it," David Kemper explains. "When we saw the rough cut, it struck all of us that they had gone so fast

into that tough place that there was nowhere to get to for acts two and three. It was really intense — they'd have to be having sex atop the Empire State Building by the end of act four if they kept going! So we re-edited to make the best episode."

One of the more unusual concepts to surface in this story had started off as one of Kemper's file card ideas: 'D'Argo gets plugged into Pilot's den, and D'Argo becomes Pilot'. "We were sitting there working out the part we wanted Stark to play, and I suggested giving that idea to Stark," Kemper recalls.

Dave Elsey was particularly impressed with Mark Mitchell as Mu-Quillus. "He was one of the most amazing guys we ever had in the make-up seat," the Creature Shop supervisor recalls. "He would sit in the chair and say, 'Good morning', and then fall asleep instantly, and not wake up until we'd finished the make-up. Then he'd go off and do his acting, come back, and fall asleep to the point of literally snoring while we took the make-up off!"

"Dave whipped up something for Mu-Quillus to wear on his hands, like glowing embers, that Mark absolutely fell in love with," Ian Barry adds. "Mu-Quillus suddenly developed a Shakespearean fondness for gesturing!" ∎

Opposite page: Mu-Quillus and Sierjna.

Above: Stark becomes Talyn's Pilot.

SCRATCH 'N' SNIFF

Written by: Lily Taylor	Guest cast: Francesca Buller (Raxil), Tamblyn Lord
Directed by: Tony Tilse	(Fe'Tor), Laura Keneally (Theiadh), Anthony Martin (Mitols), Milan Keyser (Sarl), Jaye Paul (Heska Tinaco), Julia Trappe (Blue Girl), Rachel Sheriff (Green Girl)

anished from Moya by Pilot, the crew find themselves at a party in a bar, where they intend to drink and dance the night away. The next morning, Crichton and D'Argo awaken to find themselves in a shop window in a precinct, with all their money gone. Raxil, an alien spiv, tells them that Chiana and Jool are missing, and in danger. Crichton and D'Argo are sceptical until she leads them to a Hangi, who shows them the events of the previous evening. Chiana and Jool appear to have been captured by a local villain, Fe'Tor, but when D'Argo goes to their rescue, he discovers that they are having a wonderful time, accepting Fe'Tor's hospitality freely. But things soon take a turn for the worse in Fe'Tor's basement, where he plans to extract a narcotic drug from their body essences...

> **Chiana to D'Argo**
>
> "They're gonna write songs about how you guys tore this place up."

"The script for 'Scratch 'n' Sniff' went through a lot of permutations trying to get the right tone," recalls David Kemper. "It's really hard to write that kind of whimsical fun, and have it make sense and be serious, all at the same time. Tony Tilse got *Austin Powers* in his head, and we realised that we had this intense piece about something very serious that also had a lot of comedy to it."

"It was a challenge as a director," Tilse admits. "There are a lot of times when you work on a show and everything goes right, and there are a whole lot of times when things don't quite click into place. While we were shooting it, it was a real struggle to find out what this beast was, and then David pointed out that it was being told from Crichton's point of view."

"There were so many characters involved that you wanted to freeze

ENCOUNTERS: HANGI

A mantis-like creature with removable eyes. His optic nerves continue to record and send back images even after they are separated from his body. For a fee, he will allow customers to put one of his tentacles up to their own eye, enabling them to view his optic memory banks and see a three-dimensional image of events he has witnessed.

frame when you first met them, and put a caption saying 'Bimbo' or 'Bad Guy'," Kemper explains. "When we saw the rough cut, we realised it needed something extra."

"The face of that episode changed completely in post-production," post supervisor Deb Peart says. "Tony and the editor Wayne Le Clos locked themselves away for a couple of weeks and produced a little bit of editing magic." Ben Browder points out that he and Tilse had some inkling of the eventual solution during filming. "It was always in the back of our head," he says. "We had to meld the two elements of the dark and light together. We were thinking of a *Pulp Fiction* motif, or *Lock, Stock and Two Smoking Barrels.* You're looking at a way to tell a story in a frag-mented but cohesive style, that embraces two themes that don't necessar-ily tie together well."

"We basically went out and stole the time to film the wraparound sequence we ended up using — it was like guerrilla film-making," Kemper adds. "The production company was saying that we couldn't have another minute on it, but we walked into Pilot's den, the puppeteers were game, and we shot the scenes."

'Scratch 'n' Sniff' allowed Francesca Buller to create another memo-

Above: Crichton and D'Argo assess the situation.

Next page: Mitols persuades D'Argo to leave Fe'Tor's house.

rable alien. "We knew it was a Joe Pesci kind of character, and it's a part that's very difficult to play," Kemper says. "But we knew that Fran could pull it off effortlessly — she's got a really advanced sense of humour." Kemper offered the actress the role on her birthday, and she jumped at it. "I love working with Anthony and Ben, and together they're just fabulous," Buller says. "I loved it when Anthony had to 'hit' me — he's hysterical and just lovely."

Although Buller based her accent on the cockney tones heard in Guy Ritchie's films, some of her actual dialogue came from closer to home. "They gave everything that I say in the writers' room to Raxil," David Kemper complains jokingly. "When the pages came through, I thought the words looked really familiar!"

Anthony Simcoe loved the opportunity to get away from the studio. "It was just so nice to get out and cruise on Marubra Beach and then hit a night-club," he laughs. He also got a chance to demonstrate another side to D'Argo, with his drug-induced 'Dandy D'Argo' persona. "When we shot it, I did a different voice," he recalls, "but we really needed to keep reminding people that it was D'Argo, so unfortunately we had to go and put the normal voice back in ADR." ∎

INFINITE POSSIBILITIES
PART 1: DAEDALUS DEMANDS

Written by: Carleton Eastlake **Directed by:** Peter Andrikidis	**Guest cast:** Kent McCord (Jack Crichton), Magda Szubanski (Furlow), Thomas Holesgrove (Alcar), Patrick Ward (Zylar)

Talyn discovers a wormhole through which Earth is visible. Crichton knows that this is a signal from the Ancients, and he's not surprised when the alien in the form of his father Jack appears on the bridge. Jack reveals to Crichton that the Ancients left a residual link within his mind, through which they have summoned him. Jack goes on to inform Crichton that another alien race is using a duplicate module to experiment with an unstable wormhole, and accuses him of sharing the secrets of the Ancients' technology with a third party. Assisted by the Scorpius clone, Crichton realises that the only suspect could be Furlow, the mechanic to whom he gave his research on Dam-Ba-Da. When Rygel recognises the pilot of the duplicate module as a Charrid, a race who are ancient foes of the Hynerians, Crais adds that the Charrids are now allied with the Scarrans. Returning to Dam-Ba-Da in search of Furlow, the crew come under Charrid attack…

> **Rygel to Stark**
>
> "Perfect. The half-blind leading the blind."

"Rockne always said, 'Let's make sure we don't lose sight of people,'" David Kemper recalls. "He always saw Crichton and Aeryn as an epic, mythic love story." It's a love story that has a tragic conclusion at the end of this suitably epic two-parter.

"The ultimate moral choice for Crichton is either to go home and endanger the universe, or destroy his means of ever going home, sacrificing himself to stay and defend his friends," Carleton Eastlake explains. "David thought, 'Great!', because we had to kill one of the Crichtons — so he could die doing just that."

The scope of the story came from Eastlake's interpretation of Scorpius's

ENCOUNTERS: CHARRIDS

A particularly sadistic race, well-suited to war, possessing an extremely high tolerance for pain. A thousand cycles ago, they invaded Hynerian space, leaving a billion dead, and the two races still despise each other with a passion. They are eager and persistent fighters, and at present, the Charrids are allied with the powerful Scarran Imperium.

comment to Crichton that wormholes could be used to conquer worlds. "I could see that you could use them to sneak behind enemy lines, but what was dangerous about them other than that? Then I realised controlling wormholes meant that you could plant one in a sun, so you'd have a plasma cannon that could destroy worlds. I do know quite a bit about science, but who knows how that would actually work!"

During the planning stages, Kemper and the writing staff soon agreed that one episode would not give sufficient time to serve the various elements of the story. "Carleton was saying how this really should be a two-parter," Kemper recalls, "so I made the decision that it *was* a two-parter, and we re-worked it from that moment on."

One practical result of that decision was that two different directors handled the two halves of the story. "I shot the first seven days, and then Ian Watson did the second seven," Peter Andrikidis recalls. "We had a couple of scenes that crossed over, when Crichton turned into Scorpius again, and Ian took over from that point."

When the location for Dam-Ba-Da was selected, in the sand dunes south of Sydney, Eastlake realised that "it was gigantic, and there was no way that one person, or one Hynerian, could defend it. That's when I came up with the automatic cannons on the roof. We gave Rygel a big role, so that Crichton, Aeryn

and Jack could have their scenes, and Stark and Crais could recapture Talyn — there was only Rygel left to hold off the Charrids." Team Rygel relished the opportunity. "Rygel got a gun!" Tim Mieville enthuses. "You had him looking in the distance and then looking close at the controls, which looked great and worked really well I thought."

Wayne Pygram initially looked forward to shooting at Luna Park, a funfair on Sydney's north shore that was about to be closed down. "I'd never been on a rollercoaster before," he says, "and I thought I'd be fine." However, fifteen or so takes later, "I was slowly starting to feel a bit funny," Pygram admits. "I was in the Michael Schumacher gear, and on one of the takes, I came out of myself, and looked down over the harbour, the Opera House and the Harbour Bridge, and it was beautiful. Then I got off — and I wasn't feeling good at all. Sure enough, I found a garbage bin just in time…"

Luna Park was Andrikidis's suggestion. "The scene was supposed to be shot on the water at Homebush, but I thought that was boring," the director comments. "Getting on that rollercoaster was a great example of the writers running with an idea and enhancing it."

"We knew we were bringing back a couple of great guest actors – Magda as Furlow, and Kent McCord as the Ancient," sums up David Kemper. "We had a really good story — but the key to it was getting to Crichton dying…" ■

Opposite page:
Crichton and Aeryn
prepare to attack the
bunker.

Above: *Crichton and*
Harvey's final
confrontation at
Luna Park.

INFINITE POSSIBILITIES
PART II: ICARUS ABIDES

Written by: Carleton Eastlake **Directed by:** Ian Watson	**Guest cast:** Kent McCord (Jack Crichton), Magda Szubanski (Furlow), Thomas Holesgrove (Alcar), Noel Hodda (Charrid Leader 2)

With only Stark and a blinded Crais on the ship, Talyn is boarded by a Scarran advance scout, while on Dam-Ba-Da's surface, Jack helps Crichton finally banish the neural clone from his mind. Rygel is lying wounded in the gun turret, as hordes of Charrids threaten the base. In response to the urgency of their situation, Jack unlocks the final secrets of wormhole technology in Crichton's brain, without which they will be unable to complete their task. It becomes a race against time to keep the Charrids from the door while Crichton and Jack complete a Displacement Engine that will be sufficiently powerful to knock out the Scarran Dreadnought. However, when Crichton leaves Jack to put the finishing touches to their creation, Furlow reveals her true colours, shooting Jack, and letting her allies, the Charrids in...

> **Furlow to Crichton**
>
> " Always be the one to walk away while the hero dies."

"I needed the audience to absolutely, totally, one hundred per cent believe that this Crichton was the real one," David Kemper says, "because it was true. And as soon as we were sure that they did — I knew I could go ahead and kill him! I knew I wanted to let the audience fall in love with the romance, and let Crichton and Aeryn really be together. By the time you got to the end, you know these two so loved each other, that you know he was real. This Crichton wasn't a mirage, it was our guy, flesh and blood."

Although Crichton's death overshadows the whole of the two-parter, the cast enjoyed working on the action sequences that permeated the story. "Running down the sand dunes and across these huge explosions was a real treat, but also a little scary as well," Lani Tupu recalls. "Ben ran so fast that he actually pulled his hamstring!"

Browder remembers it all too well: "They sent me to a doctor, she asked me what had happened, and I explained that there was this bunker with a bunch of aliens, explosions going off everywhere, and I was carrying a gun in one hand, and a grenade in the other. I could see the doctor reaching for the psychiatrist's number — I thought the production had told her I was an actor from a science fiction show!"

"A lot of the battle got moved outside and really expanded," Carleton Eastlake explains. "What was going to be a space battle between the shut-

tle and a Prowler turned into the dune buggy battle." Something which provided Browder and Claudia Black with a great deal of fun: "It was one of the best days of my shooting career," Black claims. "In one sequence, I had to stand up, untethered, while Ben was driving at over 100 km/h. Obviously his background in rally cars came in handy!"

Crichton's death allowed not only closure for the characters, but a foray into a danger not exclusive to the Uncharted Territories. "Crichton's demise was actually inspired by a real historical event — the first death in the nuclear programme," Eastlake reveals. "He was the guy who saw the blue flash — he was exposed directly to the radiation from a critical reaction. Not many people who see that blue light shimmer across a reactor with their unaided vision survive the experience."

And Crichton doesn't. "I think Claudia does particularly fantastic work in the deathbed scene," director Ian Watson says. "There's great work from Ben, too. You don't know when he dies. There's a three or four second pause where he ceases, and his eyes are still open. I told him that it would be really tricky for him to die with his eyes open, because we'd want

Above: Crichton-Scorpius tries to persuade Aeryn to shoot.

Next page: Crichton and Aeryn man the dune buggy.

to cut to him, and he couldn't blink. We nailed it though, that moment when he actually dies. There's a fantastic cut from Crichton to Aeryn, and it's the moment when Claudia sees the light go out in his eyes and lets her grief overtake her. I think that five seconds of television is the finest work I've ever done on the show."

"Poor Ben," Black adds. "I was a blubbering mess in the scene, and I ended up covering him in snot and tears and everything — it was quite unromantic. There's that shocking moment where she's not sure if he's gone or not, then closes his lids, and then she hesitates, puts her hands over her mouth and isn't sure what to do. I think I even shed a tear when I watched it back."

"When that John Crichton dies, it's a death that all the characters care about," Ben Browder says. "It affects not only Aeryn; Crais, Stark and Rygel are all profoundly affected. You'll never take that away from the characters who are present at the time, or from the audience. There's no cheat involved. It's not *It's A Wonderful Life*. We put the characters and the audience through the wringer, and took the show into an area story-wise that most series will never go." ■

Written by: David Kemper **Directed by:** Andrew Prowse	**Regular cast only**

hilst conducting a test in D'Argo's ship, the Luxan gets into an argument with Crichton, accusing him of interfering. The dispute escalates, culminating in D'Argo pushing Crichton into a pile of crates, rendering him unconscious. As he does so, the Growler emits a blast wave which knocks D'Argo off his feet, and cripples all the systems on board Moya that were active at the time. With Moya and Crichton still unconscious, the crew discover that the alien ship is on a countdown to self-destruct. The hanger doors cannot be opened, and the crew's only chance for survival is stopping the countdown. Meanwhile, Crichton is fighting for his life, and the neural clone knows that he too will die.

Crichton

" God, I love science fiction."

Trying to give Crichton a reason to live, the clone suggests that he should take revenge on D'Argo, and in his weakened mental state, Crichton finds himself battling his friend in an animated world…

(Turn to the 'Script to Screen' section for a detailed look at the making of this episode.) ∎

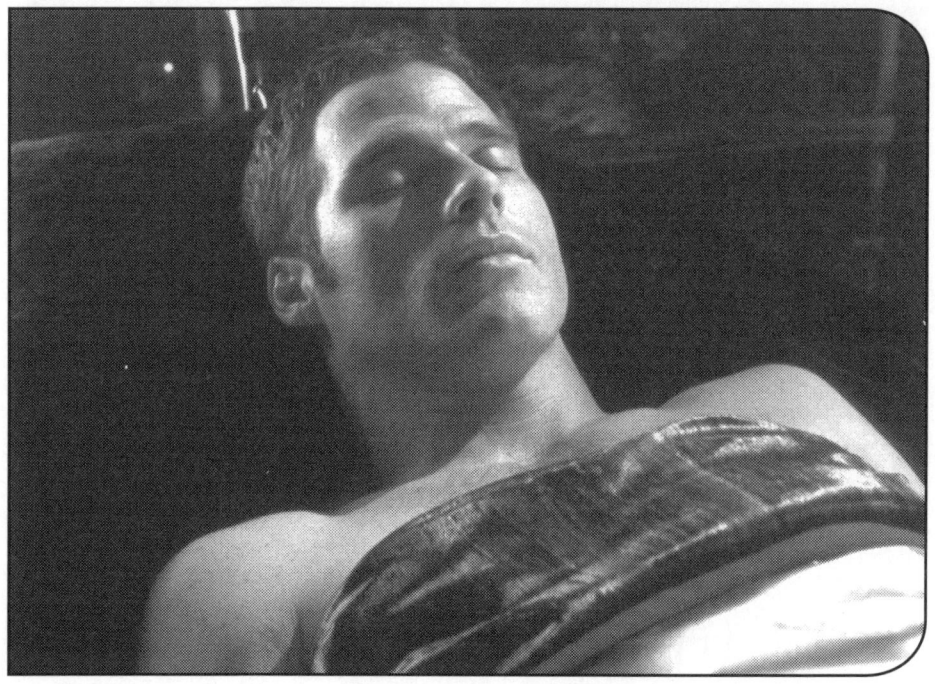

THE CHOICE

Written by: Justin Monjo **Directed by:** Rowan Woods	**Guest cast:** Linda Cropper (Xhalax Sun), John Gregg (Talyn Lyczac), Stephen Shanahan (Tenek), Raj Ryan (Hotel Owner)

In mourning for Crichton, Aeryn visits the planet Valldon, whilst Stark, Crais and Rygel argue over who knows what's best for their friend. Stark believes that the purpose of Aeryn's visit is to contact Crichton through the mystics who inhabit the planet. However, while drowning her sorrows, and apparently haunted by the ghost of Crichton, Aeryn contacts one of the locals, requesting communication not with her dead lover but with her father, Talyn Lyczak. Her intermediary comes to her hotel room, and reveals that he in fact is Talyn. Concerned about Aeryn, Stark and Rygel head down to the planet, but Stark is distracted when he keeps hearing the voice of Zhaan. He is brought back to reality when he spots Xhalax Sun lurking in Aeryn's hotel...

Aeryn to Crais

"If I squeeze my eyes closed tightly enough, you could be someone else."

"I told David Kemper that I really wanted something to sink my teeth into," Claudia Black says. "I was being greedy because I've had a great season, but I said I'd love an episode that was really Aeryn-driven." Black's request fitted with Kemper's plans. "As soon as Justin knew that we were going to kill Crichton, he said that Aeryn would be ready to commit suicide," he explains. "He wanted to write an episode that dealt with the fact that her boyfriend had died."

Black worked with Monjo and director Rowan Woods to create an episode that Black admits "ran the risk of alienating the audience." "Claudia and I love to work together," Woods says, "and to push her to those places is exciting and heart-wrenching at the same time. I was very jazzed about 'The Choice': the design represented an enormous challenge, because it obviously referenced *Blade Runner* to a certain extent, but it also represented a more gothic tradition of film-making."

Kemper describes Black's performance as a "tour-de-force", and Woods feels that this is a result of the daring choices the actress made. "It's quite astonishing, because she could have made a lot of conventional, tear-jerking choices, but she didn't," he says. "She played everything the opposite way to what you'd expect, and that was due to her very serious and rigorous homework in the weeks preceding the shoot. Claudia will really explore the opposite way to play things if she thinks it's the real, plausible, logical way to go. She'll turn the rules of drama on their head."

Woods points out that 'The Choice' is not simply about Aeryn

mourning her dead lover. "It's more a really interesting profile of some-body in denial and coming out of it," he says. "When Aeryn turns her back on ghost Crichton, she's resolving that story."

Above: *The unhelpful hotel owner.*

'The Choice' also gave a great deal of work to the puppetry team, as Rygel came to the fore. "Rowan went to a lot of trouble to do the scenes in the mar-ketplace down in the foyer of the hotel," Tim Mieville recalls. "It was full-on for us in terms of getting Mat McCoy and his team moving through all those other characters — Rygel's just the tip of an iceberg of two or three people being wheeled underneath!"

Next page: *The Seer and Talyn Lyczac.*

"I love it when Rygel is a character of integrity, and not just doing his Dr Smith thing," Woods says, referring to the manipulative schemer from *Lost in Space*. "He has some beautiful moments, especially when he's trying to con-vince Aeryn to get off the ledge."

The Creature Shop also created the Seer. "Mario Halouvas did a lovely job with that," praises Sean Masterson. "I think the Seer is incredibly 'human', while being utterly alien at the same time," Andrew Prowse adds. "Where you

come unstuck is where you've got outrageous big pieces of plastic, with clunky mouths and lifeless eyes that can only really communicate clichés. The genius of what Dave Elsey does is to create aliens that you can register subtleties with — and subtleties are what *Farscape* is all about." "Maybe the Seer knows something that we don't know," David Kemper hints. "I don't discount that. Between the Seer and Stark, you never quite know what's out there."

Linda Cropper enjoyed her final appearance on the series to date. "I liked the Greek tragedy element to it," she notes. "It had to be a fairly remarkable conclusion for Aeryn and her mother, and it had to be a very cathartic scene — which it certainly turned out to be!"

'The Choice' was Paul Goddard's final episode of the year as well, as the actor went to appear in a play at Sydney Opera House. "He gave a magnificent performance here," says Kemper. "He wasn't going to be in the rest of the season, so we came up with the idea of the mask at the end. The whole episode closes things off, and sets us up for the next story. Remember, there's always darkness before the dawn..." ∎

FRACTURES

| **Written by:** Rockne S. O'Bannon | **Guest cast:** Kate Beehan (Hubero), Matt Doran (Markir |
| **Directed by:** Tony Tilse | Tal), Thomas Holesgrove (Naj Gill) |

xpecting the arrival of Talyn, the crew of Moya are surprised when the docked transport pod reveals its occupants to be a Scarran, a female Hynerian, a Nebari and a barely conscious Peacekeeper tech, whom they welcome aboard cautiously. They were the subjects of Peacekeeper weaponry experiments, and their other comrade, a Boolite, has been smashed into pieces — although it is still alive. When the crew of Talyn does arrive shortly afterwards, excitement runs high amongst the Moya crew. Crichton races to be reunited with Aeryn, but is surprised and confused by her bare acknowledgement of him, until Crais explains the events on Dam-Ba-Da. He also hands Crichton Stark's mask, which contains a message for Crichton from his other self. But before he can hear it, Pilot interrupts to announce that "somebody aboard Moya just broadcast a distress call to the Peacekeepers…"

> **Orrhn to Rygel**
>
> "What's their plan?"
>
> "Oh, they're gonna kill you, bitch."

"I have lots of grey hairs," admits David Kemper, "but 'Fractures' didn't give me much grey hair at all! I warned Rock that he was in trouble, because he had to bring the two crews together and have all these people talking to each other, show what Crichton's going to do with Aeryn, and what she feels about him. Plus, as well as all that, he had come up with his own 'B' story of the Boolite. That's a lot for one script!"

The reunion of the crews "was a major thrust for me in the script," Tony Tilse points out. "I talked to Ben about it, and he was really clear about what he wanted to say, and Claudia had a very definite idea of what she wanted to do with Aeryn as well."

Black felt that Aeryn should simply walk straight past the excited Crichton. "It would cause her so much pain to look at him that she couldn't

ENCOUNTERS: BOOLITE

A sentient, peaceful species whose body parts can survive independently of the main body for up to half a cycle. They are self-healers; once dismembered parts are reattached, their healing process is extremely fast. They have a much higher metal content than most species and also have an incredible directional memory — they are like living maps.

do it," she says, "but we had to honour those words in the dialogue. He runs in like a teenage boy, and she blows him off and walks out of the room. He's left reeling from a response he wasn't expecting. We added in little moments to highlight the awkwardness of the situation — there's a long shot from Crichton's point of view of the back of Aeryn's head. He keeps looking to her for a response which she's not giving." Browder agrees: "It's a very difficult scene for both characters. How do you deal with someone who has that look on their face, knowing you'll shatter their world?"

The newcomers to the ship included the first sighting of a female Hynerian. "It's basically Rygel in drag!" Tony Tilse admits of Rygel's lover. "Terry Ryan had put her in a red boa, but she was supposed to be a soldier," David Kemper adds. "By the time it all came together and we saw the first dailies, we just figured that she looked like a grand old Hollywood actress or something!" Fiona Gentile provided the voice for Orrhn on the studio floor. "It was an almost strident cockney voice," Tim Mieville recalls. "It was a bit of a shock to hear the final voice that was dubbed in afterwards — it was so sedate!"

O'Bannon also created a new kind of Scarran. "They're all portrayed as very brutish, guttural guys, and I wanted to do one who's not the same — he's not soft and gentle, but not quite as hard," he explains. Thomas Holesgrove enjoyed the experience of playing Naj Gill. "The design was fitted much closer to the head and the body," he reveals, "and I did like the extra element to the character. Once he was healed, he didn't have any interest in pursuing the usual seek-and-destroy Scarran objective. He's just trying to survive."

Reconstructing the Boolite threw Jool and Crais together, and Tammy MacIntosh and Lani Tupu had fun with the scene where they both scream. "It was like performance art," MacIntosh recalls. "The camera rolled, we took a pause, looked at each other," Tupu adds, "and looked back again, looked behind us — then screamed at the same time." "I felt quite jazzed by that because there was a chemistry there," Tilse comments.

The episode fulfilled all the criteria Kemper had set for O'Bannon, plus one that SCI FI Channel added: "The network told me that they were taking a break after 'Fractures' for quite a long while," Kemper explains. "So we made the end a bit of a cliffhanger. Hopefully everybody would realise that something *really* good was coming..." ∎

Opposite page:
Moya's crew prepare
for a hostile arrival.

Above: True love?
Orrhn and Rygel.

I-YENSCH, YOU-YENSCH

Written by: Matt Ford	Guest cast: David Franklin (Lt Braca), Ben Mendelsohn
Directed by: Peter Andrikidis	(Sko), Anthony Hayes (Wa), Inge Hornstra (Essk),
	Salvatore Coco (Voodi), Thomas Holesgrove (Naj Gill)

oya makes a rendezvous with a medical ship, which will take Naj Gill. Chiana has a disturbing vision of Peacekeepers, and wonders if it might be about D'Argo and Rygel, who have gone to meet with Scorpius at a diner on an isolated planet. Scorpius and Braca arrive and check to ensure that D'Argo and Rygel are alone, before starting to negotiate the terms whereby Moya's crew will come on board Scorpius's Command Carrier. Jool is debating whether to join Naj Gill when Chiana has another vision, this time of her mourning Jool. Her first vision comes true as a Peacekeeper ship suddenly appears, but Talyn obliterates it. To the crew's horror, Talyn then targets the medical ship and despite their desperate pleas to stop, he destroys it. As the crew realise that drastic action will need to be taken, the party in the diner encounter problems of their own, as they are caught in the middle of an armed robbery...

Aeryn

"We started this together, Crichton. That's how we'll end it."

Fans of American film actor Al Pacino might wonder who their fellow admirer is on the *Farscape* set, what with 'I-Yensch, You-Yensch' deriving its basic scenario from two of his greatest movies. "I had an image of Rygel and Scorpius meeting in a diner," David Kemper explains, "just like Robert DeNiro and Pacino in *Heat*. I was talking to Matt Ford, and he said, 'It would be interesting if it started out like *Heat*, but halfway through it turned into a siege, like *Dog Day Afternoon*.'"

For director Peter Andrikidis, "the biggest thing was getting Ben Mendelsohn and Tony Hayes as the guest stars. Ben's well known as a phenomenal actor here in Australia, and Tony is up and coming. They took on that make-up, and they *became* those aliens. They really pushed it to the boundary, but still kept a form of reality."

ENCOUNTERS: WA AND SKO

These two robbers are of unknown race and questionable sanity. They are friends, but not so close that each would think the motives of the other above suspicion. When enraged or excited, their call is similar to that of an ape. They are not the brightest of creatures, and the slightest change of plan, or unusual situation, throws them into disarray.

Crichton and Aeryn, ready to face Infinite Possibilities.

An early design for the animated Crichton.

An early concept for the cartoon Scorpius.

This Looney Tunes-style painting influenced the final character designs.

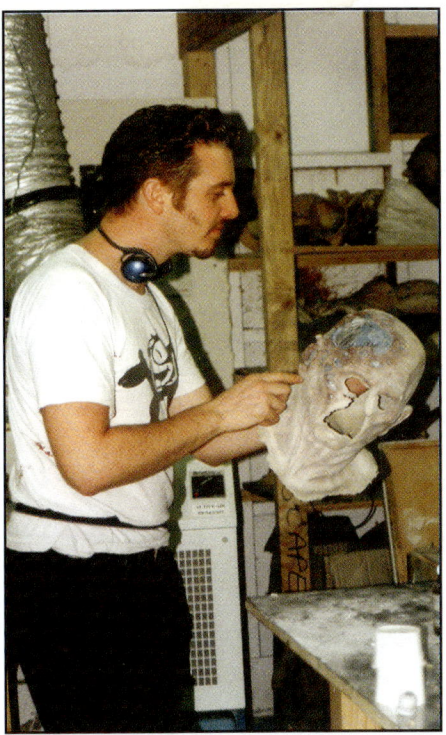

The Creature Shop's Damian Martin at work on Kaarvok's make-up.

Shane Briant as Kaarvok.

Gigi Edgley between takes on the set of 'Eat Me'.

Brett Beacham, painting a Colarta's arm.

The pirate Scarran, Naj Gill.

Scorpius's Scarran father, Wolesh.

A deadly Colarta tracker.

Tocot, the Diagnosan.

'Dandy' D'Argo.

The Seer.

Crichton-Scorpius.

Neeyala, the Pathfinder.

"It was a pleasure to work with the blue guys," Anthony Simcoe recalls. "And I had a really good time overall, even if I am lying there doing half a sit-up for days on end, handcuffed to David Franklin!" "It was a very relaxed and positive vibe on set," Franklin agrees. "It was an easy process working with Anthony — when you're enjoying something, it doesn't feel like work!"

Andrikidis admits he was concerned that he was directing an episode where Rygel was heavily featured. "We tried to design the set so that we could hide Rygel's mechanism," he admits, "but we couldn't put anything underneath the sets. That was a huge difficulty, but in the end it worked out pretty well."

"That's a testament to how comfortable the production has become, dealing with all the various elements," Rockne S. O'Bannon points out. "Early on, we had strict orders for the writers to get Rygel in one place, and use him sparingly. But now, that simply doesn't apply any more."

The story also put another piece into place for the final episodes. "We knew we would need to get Talyn onto the Command Carrier," Kemper explains, "and there was no way that they would just let this Sherman tank

Above: Scorpius and Rygel plan their next move.

Next page: Incompetent robbers Wa and Sko.

on board! We had to find a way to neuter him, and from the audience's point of view, and from Crichton's, he was neutered."

Lani Tupu notes that "Crais precipitates that. He suggests that the only way to deal with Talyn is to disarm him." But, as Kemper notes, this is part of Crais's plan. "Crais knows that any cockamamie plan that Crichton has will probably not work against Scorpius on his own home turf. He decides not to explain it to the others, but builds in a safety valve in case things go wrong — and that safety valve is Talyn. Crais is a hero — he knows that if he allows this Crichton to die, Aeryn will never be Aeryn again. Crais's love for Aeryn, and his respect for Crichton, transcends his feelings for himself. That's my definition of a hero. And, for the record, Talyn agreed."

The scenes also allowed Crichton and Aeryn to start to work together again. "But they're not looking at one another," Ben Browder notes. "It's something they often used to do, but here they don't, until the very last scene. Peter Andrikidis had to shoot us in two-shots, using deep, full length focus between us to link Crichton and Aeryn together on screen, so you could see that it was really difficult for them. He's giving her the space to come to him, but when she does, she says the one thing that he doesn't want to hear." ∎

INTO THE LION'S DEN PART 1: LAMBS TO THE SLAUGHTER

Written by: Richard Manning Directed by: Ian Watson	Guest cast: David Franklin (Lt Braca), Rebecca Riggs (Commandant Mele-On Grayza), Danny Adcock (Co-Kura Strappa), Sean Taylor (Lt Reljik), Lenore Smith (Lt Darinta Larell), Marta Dusseldorp (Officer Yal Henta), Lewis Fitz-Gerald (Tosko), Mark Mercedes (Officer Vonk)

Despite everyone's reservations, the crew of Moya decide to board Scorpius's Command Carrier. Crichton and Aeryn check the Yensch bracelets by inflicting pain on Crichton and, reassured that Scorpius feels the pain too, continue with their mission. Scorpius welcomes them and to the disgust of the Peacekeepers present, grants them full diplomatic privileges and immunity. Crichton demands that the lobotomised Talyn be brought on board, to which Scorpius agrees over Braca's dissent. Crichton begins working with Co-Kura Strappa to solve the final mysteries of the wormhole equations, while the others find themselves the target of distrust and hatred from the Peacekeepers. Aeryn especially has problems returning to the Command Carrier that used to be her home, and finds that her former friend Henta refuses to drink with her. Inevitably, tensions reach a breaking point and D'Argo finds himself at the wrong end of a knife...

> ### Crichton
>
> "I'm here on a big stinking Command Carrier, Dick Tracy's freaking neural bracelet linking me to Bram Stoker's nightmare."

"I have to think a year ahead," David Kemper says. "People have to know roughly where they're going if we're going to make pay-offs. At the end of the second season, we knew we had to bring Aeryn back to life, and we knew that we were going to split the Crichtons. Then suddenly I said that at the end of the third year, we ought to blow up the Command Carrier. But that should have a cost: someone has to die. And after a month of discussions, we decided that Crais should be the hero."

The other central element was that Aeryn and Crais were coming home. "David pointed out to me that it was going to be weirdest for those two," Claudia Black recalls. "They grew up in this environment. There were certain things that Aeryn had said about her life on the ship that we had to make sure we honoured. I had to remember that Aeryn's team mates had been demoted because of her defection."

Lani Tupu enjoyed hinting at the past relationship between Crais and Darinta Larell. "Until they kiss, no one really knows what's going to happen," he comments. "We just gave a sideways look at each other as we were marching up towards Scorpius, and I knew we could play with that."

'Lambs to the Slaughter' opens with a conscious homage to *Star Wars*, as the crew are greeted by Scorpius. The large hangar set débuted in 'Incubator', and was part of Kemper's plans for the year. "We spent a lot of money on that set, because we knew we'd need it for 'Into the Lion's Den'," he explains. "We couldn't build thirty rooms just for those two episodes. I asked Tim Ferrier to ensure that every time he built a new set for Talyn, it could work as a Talyn set, but at the end of the year, he could do a lighting change or a paint job, and it could become part of the Command Carrier."

The park helped demonstrate that although the Command Carrier was the headquarters of Scorpius's wormhole project, it was also home to 50,000 people. "We were introducing the Peacekeeper world, which is not necessarily what we thought it was," Ben Browder notes. "We knew that these people were going to die in the next episode," director Ian Watson adds, "so I suggested having some children in some of the scenes, running around the corridors." "It was a very foggy morning when we shot the first couple of scenes in the park," Claudia Black recalls, "and it looked quite

surreal, not like a real park at all. We were trying to shoot it without the ducks in frame!"

'Lambs to the Slaughter' also introduces a new threat to Scorpius: Commandant Grayza. "All of a sudden he's got problems," Kemper explains, "because this woman's on his ass! She wants something that he doesn't want." The addition of Rebecca Riggs to the cast pleased Anthony Simcoe, who has known her for years. "It was great to have her there, and also good to feel that the show was really going for it, with all the gang back together."

Ian Watson recalls Ricky Manning excitedly coming down to the set of 'Incubator' to forewarn him of the fight sequences: "He ran up and told me, 'We know that D'Argo is going to have a fistfight with a man with a circular saw on each hand, and we know that Crichton is going to fly around with a jetpack!' I remember thinking, 'Great! I can work with that!'"

At the end of the episode, Scorpius plays his final trump card. "He's been extending the hand of friendship all the way through," Ben Browder points out, "but by the end he has to resort to the strong arm, and threaten my home world to achieve what he wants..." ■

Opposite page:
Scorpius welcomes
Crichton aboard the
Command Carrier.

Above: *D'Argo,*
Chiana, Jool and
Rygel are held prisoner.

INTO THE LION'S DEN
PART II: WOLF IN SHEEP'S CLOTHING

Written by: Rockne S. O'Bannon **Directed by:** Rowan Woods	**Guest cast:** David Franklin (Lt Braca), Danny Adcock (Co-Kura Strappa), Lenore Smith (Lt Darinta Larell), Marta Dusseldorp (Officer Yal Henta), Sheridan Rynne (Brenna), Terrence Hepburn (Armak)

With Scorpius threatening Earth, and Grayza's visit throwing everyone into confusion, Crichton realises that there is only one option left — to blow up the Command Carrier. While Aeryn works on plans to evacuate as many of the 50,000 people on board as possible before the explosion, Crais goes to investigate any changes that Scorpius might have made to the Carrier's systems, but finds that he is no longer allowed access to Talyn. Crichton and Co-Kura start to unravel the missing equations from the wormhole data, just as Crais makes his demands to Scorpius. In return for a promise of restitution of rank, and access to repair Talyn's systems, he seemingly betrays his former shipmates and reveals Crichton's plan to Scorpius...

> **Crichton to Scorpius**
>
> "Flying through wormholes ain't like dusting crops, farmboy."

"I read Rockne's script, and was blown away by it immediately," says director Rowan Woods. "The first thing that came to mind was not just the epic nature of what happens in visceral terms, but also the drama, and just what's at stake here. Crichton's great speech at the end about 'one evil at a time' typifies it — the story is really about the consequences of a military mission on the peaceful people on the other side. At the end Scorpius, who's usually this heinous, evil figure, is melancholy and not vengeful."

"Once you're inside the Evil Empire, you realise that there's an ongoing ambiguity of good and evil," notes Ben Browder. "Crichton and Scorpius have come to respect each other as adversaries," David Kemper adds. "They've learned to look at each other in a new way. It didn't make sense that they'd hate each other for ever."

According to Kemper, O'Bannon called to say he was writing the best *Farscape* script he'd ever written. "We worked back and forwards with Ricky on episode twenty to make sure we took stuff and made it pay off in Rock's episode," Kemper adds. "We wanted to have the statue in the park fall through the ceiling into the corridor, to tie up that the park was on the ship. That didn't come off — but that's where Rowan got the idea of the water."

"We only had one go at the waterwall," Wayne Pygram recalls. "When the producers and half the office staff are there to watch a scene, you know that something special is about to happen! There were chairs out — it was like doing theatre. I didn't feel pressured, but suddenly I realised that all the tread had worn off my boot. The water was up to my knees, and I stepped on something on the floor under the water. I almost went over, but I knew if I did, the shot was dead, and we couldn't do it again! So I moved slowly and in a very deliberate way, which looked great, fortunately."

"The real key to that stunt is that we had our star right in front of the camera," Woods adds. "The wall explodes at the top of the staircase and several tons of water crash down towards our star!" The whole cast were caught up in the destruction of the Command Carrier. "It reminds me of the Rudyard Kipling poem 'If,'" Claudia Black says. "'If you can keep your head while all about are losing theirs...'" Anthony Simcoe's memory is somewhat more straightforward: "Blowing up that big ship was *fun*," he says.

Tupu enjoyed the nuances of his final scenes as Crais. "Just before I board Talyn at the end, there's a moment between Crais and Aeryn," he

Above: Aeryn cleans Brenna's hand.

Next page: Crichton places Co-Kura in the Aurora Chair.

recalls. "They know exactly what's going to happen, but there's not much they can actually do at that moment other than briefly acknowledge that they like each other — there's something far greater pressing."

Ben Browder suggested that Crichton should attack Crais, rather than Scorpius as scripted, when he learns of the betrayal. "Crais is standing there unguarded, and all of John's friends are in custody. Crichton has got to say to himself that Crais has done it to them again!" Browder reasons. "He let Crais out, he trusted him, and he's screwed them again. Of course, Crais and Talyn redeem themselves in the final act for many of the things they'd done which weren't so heroic. But Crichton misjudges Crais, and attacks him, which was the only course of action he could take."

"I told the producers to make it BIG," Kemper concludes. "And they apparently listened, because we spent a bunch of money on this episode! By the time you get to the end of the season everyone is exhausted, and the only way you're going to get something good out of them is to really challenge them. So we did. There were crowds, explosions, loads of CG, the emotional stuff for Crichton and Aeryn — and Crais got his revenge. Poor Scorpius — he never had a chance with both Crichton *and* Crais working against him." ■

DOG WITH TWO BONES

| Written by: David Kemper | Guest cast: Kent McCord (Jack Crichton), Melissa Jaffer |
| Directed by: Andrew Prowse | (Old Woman) |

A s Moya arrives at the Leviathan burial ground to deposit the remains of Talyn, Crichton is besieged by visions of his life if he returned to Earth, and his fears of whether Aeryn would fit in. Everyone is preparing to leave Moya once Talyn has been buried, but first they have to deal with another Leviathan, who tries to prevent Moya from entering the area. A mysterious old woman has remained on Moya after all the other refugees from the Command Carrier have left, and she drugs Crichton in an effort to help him see the truth he's searching for. Pilot discovers that the other Leviathan has gone mad, and has killed her Pilot. Moya refuses to accept that she will not be allowed to bury her son, and asks for the crew's help to kill the rogue...

Harvey to Scorpius

" The human subconscious is a fascinating place. Malleable. Permeable. Fallible."

"I wanted to wrap up the season with some flair," David Kemper states. "I wanted something that other shows just don't give you." To achieve that, Kemper went through weeks of what he describes as "torture". "I had a two-parter that would have ended this year but I could not make it work, because my 'B' story was Crichton fantasising about the wedding, and it kept wanting to be the 'A' story." Eventually, Kemper decided that "I'm going to give *everyone* the wedding. You read about lunatic executive producers doing something different at the last minute, and I felt really guilty. Rockne said, 'Just write a good script.'"

"We all wanted that episode to be something you could remember," Andrew Prowse confirms. "It was really tough, but we wanted a climax as good as the end of season two." Kemper realised that he had already shown the 'physical' end of the season with the explosion of the Command Carrier in the previous episode, and now he could pay off the emotional arc. "I flipped the paradigm of having the 'A' story being the main narrative and the character stuff being the 'B' story, and came up with the story of the rogue Leviathan, which was designed to be simple."

The scene between Crichton and D'Argo that cuts from D'Argo's ship, the Growler, to the dockside and back, is one of Anthony Simcoe's favourite parts of the episode. "We worked really hard at making that work," he says. "There were lots of different versions, and we ended up improvising, using long lenses and long takes. Andrew gave us a lot of looseness to perform that."

The wedding sequences took two days to shoot. "It took a while. I thought the hotel management was going to throw us out!" Prowse admits. "When Pilot arrived at the location, it was all hands on deck to get him up the stairs," Sean Masterson recalls. "Pilot doesn't get out much as you know, so to mark the occasion, we let the special effects team rig some squibs on him for the first time."

"The wedding scenes seem like such a harbinger of doom," Claudia Black comments. "I went through the old costumes, and found Katralla's wedding dress from 'Look at the Princess' — I wanted there to be a quirky resonance there of that other woman Crichton has married." Black contributed a number of ideas to the episode, including Aeryn's dying line. "We realised that even though it was the other Crichton who had said this, if this Crichton was dying, he would probably say the same thing, so he could give the line to someone dying in a fantasy," Kemper explains.

Kemper, Browder, Black and Prowse worked together on the critical final scene between Crichton and Aeryn. "We were looking for the elegant ending," Kemper says. "I wanted a mature dissolution to their rela-

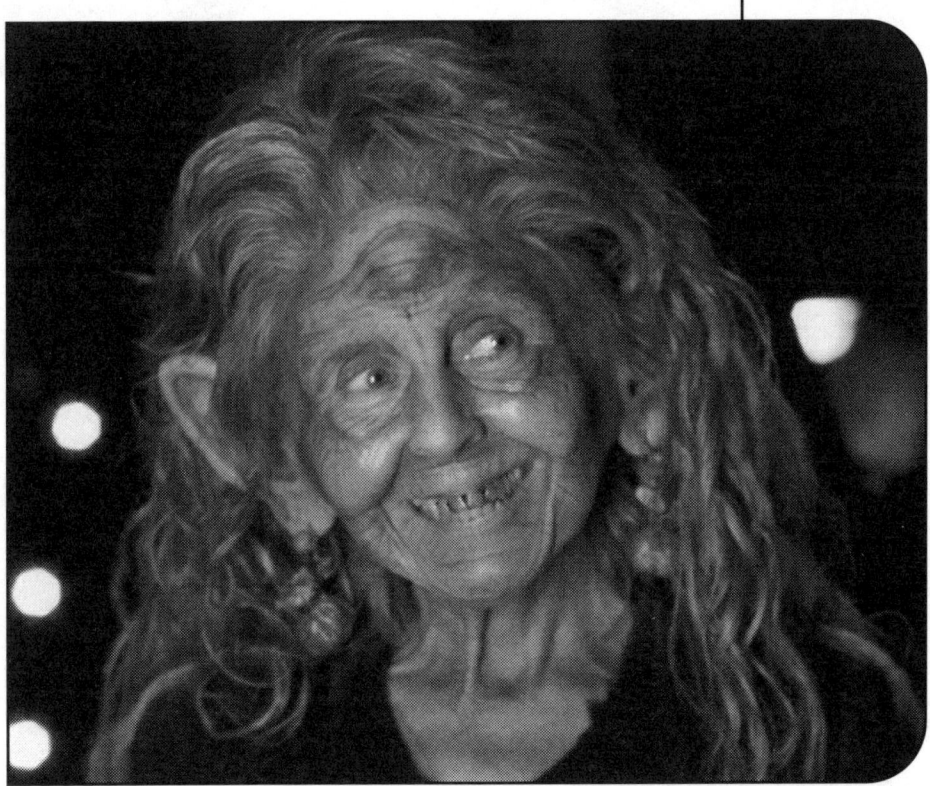

tionship and to show that they have grown." "We needed to get to a point where Aeryn left the ship," Black continues. "I suggested to David that we should have a coin toss. I said it wasn't trivialising the decision — it was so painful, they should let something else make the decision for them, because otherwise it would just hurt too much. David went with it, and I was really proud. That was the biggest contribution I've made to a story on *Farscape*."

Although the coin toss initially seemed a good way to close the season, there was more. Only four copies were made of the script page that contained the Old Woman's revelation to Crichton. "Nobody had a clue," Kemper says. "Even Ben didn't have the page until the very last minute. So they've separated, Aeryn is pregnant, Crichton finds that out, and on top of everything else, Moya gets swallowed by a wormhole. Andrew and I knew we had a final scene that worked!"

So at the end of the season, "they not only take away the girl, they take away everybody!" Ben Browder concludes. "He's left alone in space. Lost in his module, where he started off at the beginning of season one. Except this time, there ain't nobody nearby!" ∎

Opposite page:
Wedding guests Jack, D'Argo, Chiana and Jool toast their comrades.

Above: The mysterious Old Woman.

SCRIPT TO SCREEN

"I know a guy. Dr Chuck Jones wrote the book on these situations."

– John Crichton

"After the death of the Crichton on Talyn, I decided to completely catch the audience off guard. Let's face it, no one expected us to follow up the demise of our lead character with the Road Runner!"

"I t's a hell of a mix," begins Anthony Simcoe. "First, you've got the 'real' world of *Farscape*, if you can call it that. Then there's the fantasy world of what's going on in John's head, with the Scorpy clone. *Then* you've got the cartoon world on top of that!" he adds, trying to sum up the genre-defying, groundbreaking season three episode 'Revenging Angel'. "Bridging a storyline between those three very different realities was a difficult and brave task," he continues, "but it was lots of fun to work on."

"David Kemper and I must be the world's leading authorities on Chuck Jones cartoons. We've seen them all a hundred times," director Andrew Prowse maintains, referring to the legendary animator behind Road Runner, amongst many other classic Warner Bros characters. 'Revenging Angel' showed "the genius of Kemper," Prowse continues. "He will throw ideas at you out of left field. You never know if he's serious, or if it's ever going to happen. It's a cliché to talk about pushing the envelope, but he just keeps doing it — he attempts things that are apparently utterly outrageous."

The genesis of 'Revenging Angel' stretches back to the early part of *Farscape*'s second year. "Andrew and I worked on this for eleven months before anyone else had to do anything," Kemper explains. "It was in my head from the day after I conceived 'Won't Get Fooled Again' for season two. I had two really wacky ideas in a row, and I knew that we couldn't do them both in one year. We did 'Won't Get Fooled Again' first because we knew that 'Revenging Angel' was going to take forever."

The first requisite for a cartoon episode of *Farscape*? An animation house that could both provide work to the exacting standards that the production team demanded of itself, and would understand the very unusual nature of the show. Luckily, such an outfit was on their doorstep, and even had a strong link to *Farscape* in the show's resident composer, Guy Gross.

"Guy's parents run the largest animation house in the southern hemisphere," Kemper says. "Yoram Gross-E.M.-TV Studios make cartoons for the whole of Asia and Australia. I had met Guy's parents and we had become good friends. I had seen their work, and knew it was simply the best there is — so it was a no-brainer to use them. Had they not been here, and had I not known that we had access to them and they would do it, we might not have attempted 'Revenging Angel', because it would have been too difficult to find someone on the outside."

"We're the oldest animation studio in Australia," Yoram Gross's head of

production Rodney Whitham explains. "Yoram Gross was a Polish Holocaust survivor who emigrated to Australia in the late sixties, and was the first person to do an animated feature in Australia. Now, we mostly do TV series, but we also have a CD-ROM company, and a sound studio that works on features that shoot in Sydney, including *Moulin Rouge*. I met David, and it was back in October 2000 that we first discussed doing animation for an episode. I soon discovered that we're both big Looney Tunes fans."

At first Kemper's proposal did not meet with enthusiasm from all the series' producers. "People asked, 'Why do you want to make a cartoon episode?'" Andrew Prowse recalls. "'You're making a perfectly good series here — why do you want to screw it up with cartoons?' And Kemper just said, 'I want to make a cartoon episode, and it's going to be *really* cool.' Somehow, we got past everybody's objections. Every time we talked to anybody about it, they'd remind us how much money it was going to cost, how difficult it would be with scheduling, and how we didn't actually have a script when we were already talking to the cartoon people."

Executive consultant Carleton Eastlake recalls numerous evenings spent "rushing off to the animation house" during his time in Australia at the start of 2001, and Kemper and Prowse sitting up into the early hours hammering out the plot. "We had to figure it out," Kemper says. "We had to really get it together, because I had to write the cartoons long before I wrote the script for the rest of the episode. I had to know the plot well enough in outline to know what the cartoons would be, and have some inkling of how I was going to get them to fit into the whole. That was the most difficult part."

"The animation house had a hard time getting a handle on what we

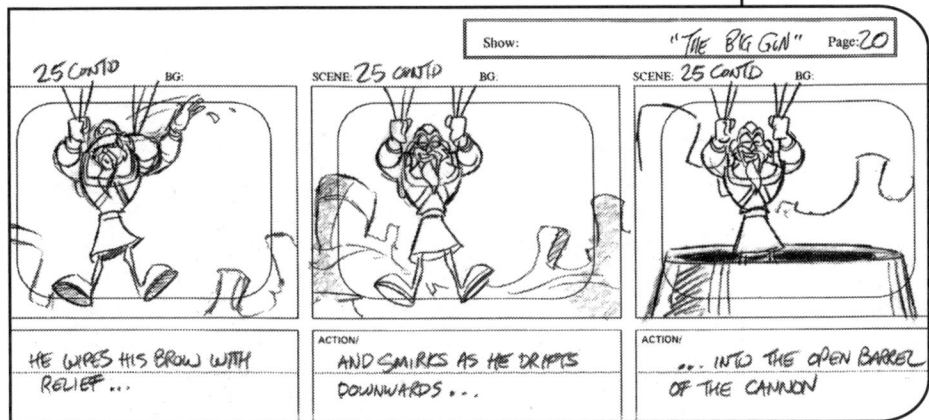

Show: "THE BIG GUN"   Page: 20

25 CONT'D   BG:

SCENE: 25 CONT'D   BG:

SCENE: 25 CONT'D   BG:

HE WIPES HIS BROW WITH RELIEF ...

ACTION/ AND SMIRKS AS HE DRIFTS DOWNWARDS ...

ACTION/ ... INTO THE OPEN BARREL OF THE CANNON

wanted," Prowse continues, and Rodney Whitham recalls numerous meetings with Kemper and Prowse "narrowing down the style of animation." At that point, Whitham called in various artists, who each came up with different designs in their own styles. "Arthur Folloy, who had worked on *Ren and Stimpy*, had more of a traditional Warner Bros look to his concept. He did a drawing of Crichton about to belt D'Argo with a hammer. We looked at a lot of different approaches, and David concluded that he definitely wanted a Looney Tunes style. He started thinking about how to incorporate that sort of Chuck Jones look, timing and movement into the script. Once we narrowed the style, we started doing more designs."

Capturing Ben Browder's likeness as Crichton caused the designers the most problems. "What's the essential feature of Ben that's going to make him recognisable?" Prowse questions. "He's a good looking guy — he doesn't have a huge nose or ears that stick out!" Whitham agrees: "He had the least amount of physical features which you can characterise. A lot of the early designs for Crichton didn't work, because they became caricature. Aeryn we hit early on because Claudia Black has a very striking look, with strong features, so she was less of a problem. D'Argo was quite easy: we hit him spot on, and then it was a matter of playing with details. We had a few variations of Scorpius: I think he works well as a cartoon character, and like D'Argo, his attire is very easy to reconstruct in animation."

By this stage, Kemper was meeting with the animators regularly, discussing the gags for the cartoon sequences, and storyboarding them until they worked to everyone's satisfaction. Then began the process of creating the animation itself, starting with animatics. "We scan the storyboard and composite them in real time, so each panel of the storyboard appears in a movie for the amount of time that the actual sequence it's illustrating would run," Whitham explains. Adjustments were made at this stage, as David Kemper began to

Page 79: *Character designs for the animated Crichton.*

Page 80: *The character reference sheet for D'Argo.*

Above: *Storyboard for the 'Big Gun' sequence.*

finalise the script of the cartoon sections and Andrew Prowse checked the timing. "We were wandering around in the dark with some kind of street map," Prowse comments of the experience, "and it was pretty lucky that we found our way out of it!"

To help them develop the animatics into line drawings, and eventually to fully rendered cartoons, the animation house needed a soundtrack from the actors, to use as a guide track. "I remember explaining to the actors what was going to happen," Prowse says. "Some of them got it, but some just looked uncertainly at me and wondered what the hell we were doing to them! What were they going to look like? Were we going to lampoon them? It shifted perspectives for a lot of the characters, and we were coming up against what people had invested in the show."

"We had no proper images of what we'd look like, or what the animators were trying to achieve," Wayne Pygram points out. "Andrew told us to 'do what you do, but as a character.' What does that mean? So I did it in a very heightened way, which is pretty outrageous, because Scorpius was somewhat heightened to begin with. I just had more fun with it."

As the animation house progressed with their work, and Kemper and Prowse refined the script and the timing of the gags, post-production supervisor Deb Peart was appointed editor of the episode. "David and Andrew asked if I'd be interested in editing it, and I said I'd love to. If I was going to manage all of

the components in post, I might as well edit it as well. At the time, I thought it would be pretty straightforward!"

Opposite page: At work in the Yoram Gross studios.

Nothing on 'Revenging Angel' was straightforward, however. While Kemper was completing his script for the live-action sections, he discussed it with Ben Browder, and heard something he didn't want to hear. "Ben said, 'This doesn't work yet,'" Kemper recounts. "I didn't understand what he meant. He wanted to make a change to the critical scene where Crichton is talking to Scorpius about why he wants to live. Initially, it wasn't about Crichton being in love with Aeryn, it was something else. Ben argued that it *had* to be about Aeryn — the Crichton on Moya is thinking about Aeryn."

As soon as Browder said that, the penny dropped for Kemper. "That was the key to making this episode work," he says. "Now there's a real emotion to it, and it's about Aeryn. Ben was saying that the audience was going to hate this Crichton. They would love the guy on Talyn, whose love for Aeryn was so evident when he died, but this Crichton, well, we were purposely keeping his feelings vague. We even talked about potentially giving him another lover in the interim, maybe have him meet someone on a planet, but then decided that he had to stay 'clean'!"

As well as monitoring the progress of the animation, and keeping up his regular work supervising post-production on the series, Andrew Prowse somehow found time to direct the live-action sections of 'Revenging Angel'. "The reason the episode works is not because it's funny, but because it has an essential core that is dead serious," he explains. "The comedy components and the fantasy are hung together through that central core. You know *why* these strange sequences are occurring. Without that, you'd have nothing, just a bit of frippery."

The 'serious' scenes gave Tammy MacIntosh a chance to show new sides to Jool. "I loved the bit with D'Argo on the Growler," she says. "Andrew knows me so well that he won't let me get away with anything, and he really makes me work!" Prowse remembers the day well: "Before we did that scene I told Tammy that I really wanted to make a strong connection between Jool and D'Argo. We did a take where she cried, and I asked her why she'd made that decision. She said, 'I thought that's what I should do, but actually it didn't feel quite right.' So I explained that what Jool was doing was trying to get D'Argo to respect her. The next take she did was amazing. She zeroed in on that, and made it much more moving than just watching somebody cry." Gigi Edgley also enjoyed her 'conversations' with Jool over Crichton's unconscious body. "By the end of that scene, Ben had a headache," she recalls. "Despite the fact he was wearing ear plugs!"

"To this day, the single all-time funniest performance in *Farscape* is from Anthony, when D'Argo walks down the aisle towards Crichton for the second time," David Kemper laughs. "He steps forward. You hear a snap and he goes, 'FNNAHR!' When we showed it to people, we used to stop the film

and ask them what just happened. Everyone always said, 'He stepped on a bear trap!' Everyone knows, because they've seen cartoons before! Anthony conveys 'bear trap', yet no one sees the trap until afterwards. That's how good his grimace is — the scene took take after take, because he was working to get it just right."

"It was interesting filming that," Andrew Prowse adds. "I was stepping outside my field of expertise, shooting a sort of live-action cartoon. I had a lot of fun, but I wondered how people did it. How do you shoot slapstick comedy on film?" "It was really difficult to find the right style to play it," Simcoe admits. "I've got images of me walking up and down that aisle I can't remember how many times! I was doing lots of different pratfalls. Some of the takes were actually funnier than the ones in the episode I thought, but they didn't fit in with the style we were aiming for."

Because 'Revenging Angel' was based around the Moya crew, "Aeryn wasn't supposed to be in the episode," Claudia Black recalls. "But David asked me if I'd like to do a little sequence as a cartoon Aeryn opposite the live-action Crichton, and I said 'Absolutely!'" Inspiration for Aeryn's costume changes came from many sources. "David sent an e-mail to everyone on the show asking for characters for her to transition into, because he needed twenty of them straight away," Carleton Eastlake remembers. "There were ones that they definitely wanted to have," Black continues. "We've always had the shadow of *The*

Wizard of Oz running through the show, so Dorothy was always going to be in. Marilyn Monroe was such an icon in *The Seven Year Itch* that they really wanted to do that, and combine it with her famous 'Happy Birthday, Mr President'. Cleopatra I believe was David's idea. Jessica Rabbit we all wanted to do! I think I'd suggested it very early on, and Ben definitely had. The *Baywatch* one was my idea. Originally, I'd asked if she could be running on the spot, in slow motion. There were a couple more that I recorded — I can do impersonations of a few singers, and we were trying to work them in, but we couldn't in the end. Some of the ones I did were quite difficult — I didn't grow up with Nancy Reagan, although I knew she had done the Just Say No! campaign."

When Black saw how the animated Aeryn first appeared, "I said to Andrew, 'that's the only time you're going to get me in such a skimpy outfit onscreen!' 'Exactly,' he said. 'It's a cartoon: we can do whatever we want!' Andrew asked me to come to the set, to be in the room for Ben, just so he had a point of reference, even though I couldn't be there on camera." Browder was appreciative of Black's presence — "she even stood there wearing a stunning outfit!" he recalls.

Once the live-action sequences were in the can, what Andrew Prowse describes as the "biggest post-production nightmare of the season" began. "We were editing the episode together using the rough line work animation, which is in black and white. It's moving, but it's very difficult to get an idea of what you're really looking at," Deb Peart points out. "As we were cutting, we were starting to get an idea of what the episode was going to look like, but it was only after we'd actually finished editing that we received the finished animation sequences and put them in."

"We had the live-action film cut together, with holes for the cartoons," Kemper elaborates, "even though the cartoons were started six months before we shot the live-action stuff. We were thinking that if the cartoons sucked, we were dead! We shot extra footage just in case the cartoons didn't work, so we would be able to do something else — maybe go back and shoot another day and pick up some more scenes. We had live-action footage that was good, but it was the connective tissue — without the cartoons, it didn't make any sense. While we were waiting for the animation, we were just desperate. Andrew and I were seeing our careers flash in front of our eyes!"

"Yoram Gross were still struggling to get things in because of late script changes," Deb Peart explains. "There were script changes to the two sequences that involved live action and animation together," Rodney Whitham adds. "They were the last sequences that we got, and they were the most complex ones to construct."

"We knew there was visual effects work to be done to those sequences once we got them back," Peart continues. "I think Animal Logic turned around close to forty shots in the Aeryn and Scorpy sequences in a week!" Eventually,

Opposite page: The dastardly D'Argo plans his revenge.

"the cartoons came in and they were funny," Kemper says. "We knew it was going to work. We weren't thinking it was a smashing success, but at least it worked."

Opposite page:
'What's up, D'Argo?' A
post-explosion Luxan.

At that stage the edited footage was handed over to Guy Gross, who had to follow in the footsteps of Looney Tunes composer Carl Stalling. "I grew up with that kind of music," Gross points out. "It's in the blood. Being the son of animation producers, I've written all the music for their animated films, but never quite to the degree to which I did in this one. I normally write anywhere from ten to twenty minutes of music in a good, solid day. On 'Revenging Angel', I think I sometimes walked out of my office at the end of the day having written maybe thirty or forty seconds. Boy, do I now have respect for Carl Stalling. It is torturous! You've got to learn to turn on a dime musically."

Kemper is full of praise for Gross's work, which earned the composer the 'Best Music for an Animation' award from the Australian Guild of Screen Composers. "Even the transition at the end where the music goes from Looney Tunes into the *Farscape* theme was fantastic!" he enthuses. "Then the sound effects guys did their thing, and by that stage we knew: this episode *really* worked."

There was one more process needed to complete production: the actors had to go back and re-record their dialogue for the cartoon sections. "We realised that although we had gone over the top on the guide voice track, it was not actually far enough," Anthony Simcoe reveals. "We had to be really extreme, because that animated world was so extreme."

Prowse was relieved to see the completed episode. "It has that combination of music, effects, timing and lots of little bits that go to make comedy that you don't really see until it's all put together at the end," he says. "Andrew and I celebrated with a really expensive bottle of wine," Kemper adds. "We dodged the bullet. We made it. We survived one more day."

'Revenging Angel' came together through the efforts of hundreds of people. In addition to all those involved at Homebush Bay and in the post-production department at Fox Studios, Yoram Gross brought in freelance animators to join their already sixty-strong team. Jon McCoenahan, who trained all the current Warner Bros Classic animators, ensured that the timing and pace matched the original Road Runner cartoons, from which the script drew its inspiration. "It was a short, sharp learning curve for those people who had not done that sort of animation before," Rodney Whitham notes, modestly conceding that he was very happy with the results.

"It's one of my favourite episodes as producer," David Kemper concludes. "We didn't take the easy road — but then we never do. To me, that's what makes *Farscape* so good. I'm proud we went and took a chance when other shows don't take chances. Other people were telling us not to, but we ignored them. We took a chance, and you know what? It worked out *great*." ■

THE CHARACTERS

"Feeling left out, D'Argo? We're the only ones who don't have voices in our heads."

– Aeryn Sun

JOHN CRICHTON

> "When I was a kid, I dreamed of outer space. Then I got here, and I dream of Earth. And lately, none of my dreams work."

At the end of 'Die Me, Dichotomy', Crichton believes that Aeryn is dead and that Scorpius has finally won. A season later, the astronaut's journey through the Uncharted Territories has come full circle, as once again he finds himself in his module, lost in a distant part of the universe, knowing that the woman he loves is far away.

Of Crichton's emotional state during the first part of season three, Ben Browder comments: "I think he's reacting quite normally!" There's certainly a contrast to the character's increasingly erratic behaviour in season two: "He's not behaving unusually or oddly in any particular fashion. He's coping, and a certain amount of normalcy has returned." But nothing's *too* normal in *Farscape*: "He's still got Scorpy in his head, so he's a little uncertain about that," Browder concedes. "Plus, his dead girlfriend is back from the afterlife and says she loves him — but they're not going to do anything about it."

Even before the Crichtons go their separate ways, John is starting to become obsessed with wormholes, although Browder challenges the description. "He's *not* obsessed," he claims. "Wormholes are his way to get home, and one of the most powerful tools in the universe. If he doesn't figure it all out, then Scorpy is going to come and rip it out of his brain anyway. I think it's quite reasonable that he explores it. Wormholes give him a bargaining chip with all these powers of the universe that seem to be allying themselves against him. He needs to know what they are in order to be able to deal with those adversaries. And is it obsessive, if you're stuck on an island, to be trying to build a boat?"

While Zhaan's death and the massacre in '...Different Destinations' remind Crichton of his own mortality, Browder thinks that "he was coping OK up to the point of 'Eat Me', which was a particularly stressful event. D'Argo dies, Chiana dies, he thinks that the ship's going to die, and he's stuck there. Then he gets back to Moya and suddenly there are two of him! It's a completely different universe once there are two Crichtons."

While the Crichton on Talyn has the compensation of Aeryn's presence, and their growing love for each other, he also has to put up with Crais. "Rightly or wrongly, he doesn't trust Crais," Browder says. "He's not rational when it comes to that guy. Don't forget that Crichton was strapped into the Aurora Chair and nearly driven nuts, and Crais was there hitting and punching him in the face while he was being tortured! It's an image that is burned into Crichton's brain. Everyone else may forget about that image, but John Crichton does not. He does not forget that they wouldn't have had a prob-

lem in the first place, if Bialar Crais hadn't pursued them across the galaxy on an unjust cause! Why *should* he trust him?"

This Crichton gives his life to save the universe, preventing the Charrids from getting the wormhole technology. "He flourishes and becomes a hero," Browder points out, "never more so than on his deathbed. He says, 'I've never felt better.' He's trying to say, 'I don't have regrets, I'm happy here, I'd do it all over again,' and I think that's an outstanding moment. The action of being a hero, going to stop the Scarrans and the Charrids, is all easy in comparison to being on his deathbed and saying to Aeryn, 'You be happy, you matter more than anyone else.'"

The other Crichton, left on Moya without Aeryn or even his pulse pistol, is "less grounded. What was critically important, which I felt underpinned him, was that he has love and he has hope," Browder says. "He believes that things are going to work out, and he's pinned a lot of that on Aeryn, because she's the girl he loves. There were a lot of words and unspoken promises exchanged between them before she left, so he's hoping that things are going to work out for the best when she comes back. He diverts himself into the wormhole stuff — he needs to do that. He's coming to the growing realisation that he has to deal with the wormholes because they're just not going to go away!"

When Aeryn returns in 'Fractures', "the thing that has been holding him up for so long is coming back. He's eternally optimistic. But one look and two words from Aeryn, and his world disintegrates." Crichton's world continues to be turned upside down when he receives the message from his *alter ego*. "There's a beautiful moment in the way in which the two Crichtons are put back together again," Browder says. "Whatever Crichton was doing before, he now has the responsibility of his other half as well. That's a big hero moment. 'It's not just me,' he realises, 'it's him, it's her, it's the *universe*, that's what I'm going to focus on.' The rest of the season for Crichton follows through from that moment."

Along the way, Crichton starts to query his own sense of judgement. "On the Command Carrier amongst the Peacekeepers, Crichton has a problem: this is the enemy, but they're not the kind of clear-cut evil characters that he imagined back when they were chasing him around the universe," Browder says. "Plus, he had told himself that Crais had screwed them and was evil, but in the end, Crais throws all of that into question. When Scorpius makes reasonable statements, that John has messed up the universe, and the Scarrans are going to overrun everything, John has to realise that the world is not black and white. Evil is not completely evil. The entire set of circumstances of 'Into the Lion's Den' questions the validity of John Crichton's judgement in painting people as simply good or bad."

With Scorpius beaten, Crichton believes he has solved his personal dilemma. "In 'Dog with Two Bones', he manages to finally say what he wants. He has help all the way along in getting there, but to get to that point in his life is a big thing. He says to Aeryn, 'Forget Earth, forget all of that, I want you.' He makes the decision that he's *not* going to go to Earth, he's going to give the whole damn thing up. There's one thing that he wants more than anything else, and that's the girl, and maybe if he has that, everything's going to work out. So he tells her — and it doesn't work out! She plays a trump card back on him and says, 'If you love me, don't make me stay.' The timing of these things is beyond his control.

"So ultimately, the universe is conspiring to keep him from getting what he wants," Ben Browder concludes. "John Crichton's journey is a rough one, and it ain't over yet!" ■

" My life has been filled with doing what others think is right. For me, for now, this is right."

"I had an incredible season," Claudia Black says gratefully. "I had unbelievably emotional stories to tell — the relationship with Crichton and Aeryn developing, and Aeryn and her mother. They were really dramatic, juicy storylines and so that was wonderful for me."

Life turns full circle for Aeryn Sun through the third year — she begins it dead, and ends with creating a new life. Black sees her development as a continuation of the progress that she has made since the first year. "Aeryn wants to constantly move forward, avoid the emotion and try to be a soldier," she points out. Even in limbo it seems, Aeryn is still a soldier. "There's her classic comment: 'Have you come to reassign me?'" Black recalls. "Once a soldier, always a soldier! Whether she understands that she's dead and believes in 'soldier reincarnation', or whether she's in denial about death and actually thinks that this person coming through the mist is coming to take her onto her next posting, it's a lovely metaphor for who Aeryn is."

However, her return to life means that "she's become more emotionally attached," Black believes. "She can't cope with what Zhaan has done for her, and it takes her a while to come to terms with it. Her emotions are making her appreciate the loss of a life a lot more than she ever would have previously."

A number of Aeryn Sun's other cherished ideals come under fire in the early part of the year. "She gets constant reminders that the Peacekeepers are not what she was taught to believe," Black says. "It pipes back to everyone telling her that she can be so much more. Well, obviously, she can be, because everything she was taught about the Peacekeepers falls short of her expectations. I think she's also developed some of Crichton's cynicism: everything that happens in the Uncharted Territories seems somehow inextricably linked, and it's always the worst case scenario."

She does, however, maintain her ability to function as a soldier when necessary, kicking Pilot into action when he is succumbing in 'Wait for the Wheel'. "There's a nice combination of Aeryn's genuine care for him as a being, and her capacity to do what is necessary as a soldier," Black explains.

Aeryn's growth continues when the crew separates: "In 'Green Eyed Monster', Aeryn decides that she wants to have a relationship with a real person. She makes a very specific choice between Talyn and Crichton because she realises that Talyn is being a petulant child. It is a living ship, but she can never trust that Talyn will be loyal to her." Black notes that the former Peacekeeper's attitude towards Earth is changing as well. "It was my idea for

Aeryn to be learning English," she reveals. "It was a nice opportunity for intimacy between Crichton and Aeryn."

The relationship is brought to an end by Crichton's self-sacrifice in 'Infinite Possibilities', and Black is especially pleased how Aeryn comes across in Crichton's death scene. "I took her to some new places," she says. "She could show not only how much she had grown with Crichton, but also how much love had made her soften. They really do love each other in that scene. It's the biggest thing that has happened to her in the show, apart from seeing her mother."

Many of Aeryn's beliefs are challenged when she finally faces her mother, Xhalax Sun, in 'Relativity'. "Initially, I think that Aeryn is actually quite excited to meet her," Black says, "though obviously she's frightened out of her wits as well." By the time Crais has faked Xhalax's execution and Aeryn meets her again in 'The Choice', the former Peacekeeper has been through so much that it's a very different person who trades barbs with her mother. "I wanted Aeryn to be in a very dark place, where all her joy had gone, all her capacity for surprise had been eliminated, and she was forced into an arena where she just didn't trust anyone," Black explains. "She ages through the experience of seeing her mother again, and knowing that her mother wanted her to feel pain. There's a nice moment of recognition that finally passes between Aeryn and Xhalax when Aeryn accepts what must be."

Black describes Aeryn in 'The Choice' as "a person who's on the edge, desperately trying to keep it together. You get to a point where you're so in shock with everything that's happened to you, that you're not really 'there'. It was a good challenge to convey that sort of stillness, pain and numbness."

When the crews are reunited in 'Fractures', Black faced what she describes as "the two hardest words of dialogue that I've ever had to say on *Farscape*: 'Hello, John.' I was expecting that Aeryn would be so incapable of looking him in the eye that she would just walk past him. I had to accelerate Aeryn's process to the point where she was capable of looking him in the eye — but as a soldier, doing it in the most perfunctory fashion, then walking off, and him learning from that that there's something wrong. She finally admits to this Crichton that the relationship she had was everything she ever hoped for. She never imagined that love could ever be like that.

"So Aeryn decides that she's not going to let Crichton's passing stand for nothing. She's going to honour his death," Black continues. "She understands why he gave his life, and now she needs to pursue it. She doesn't really trust the other Crichton, because she can't be sure what his agenda is. He's not in a terribly good state, and he's not the John that she'd fallen in love with."

Black believes that this is part of the reason why Aeryn has to leave Moya when she realises she is pregnant. "I have to presume that Aeryn is freaked out, because she may not be certain who the father is," she says, giving her take on the revelations in the season's final minutes. "Even if it is the other John, that will still have implications, because she would want to honour him, and have the child, but at the same time she would know that the surviving John would want to rear the child as his own. She may not want him to do that, so she really needs to leave, if only to get her head sorted out."

Black sees the year as "a season of death and goodbyes for Aeryn", and she is looking forward to getting back into production: "I know there are some changes on the way, but I'll be very interested to see where Aeryn ends up at the end of season four, because, believe me, I have absolutely no idea what's going to happen!" ■

KA D'ARGO

"I have nothing, John. Wife. Son. Lover. Home. Nothing. I've been forced to manufacture distractions to keep interested in living."

"The trick with D'Argo is that the viewers can never quite settle on what they think he is," Anthony Simcoe maintains. "We always have to turn that diamond and show a new facet, and it's usually a facet that people really aren't expecting. You can 'build' human characters, and they all add up to something in the end, but my observation of working in make-up is that prosthetic characters and aliens just don't add up in the same way. You've got to keep presenting different aspects, because people don't relate to them as easily as they do to a human being. With humans, it's not necessarily the characters that you change, it's the positions you put those characters in. But with the aliens, you've actually got to keep changing the characters themselves a little bit all the time to keep them fresh, interesting and dynamic. If you're not searching for something to discover in them, you end up focussing on the fact that they're made of rubber!"

The third season provided a number of changes for D'Argo, as he discovered the treacherous relationship between his son Jothee and his lover Chiana, then focused his attention on the ship that he discovered in 'Suns and Lovers'. "I'm more proud of my work in 'Suns and Lovers' than any other episode," Simcoe states. "You get to see different shades of D'Argo in that story, and it was good to know that I had the support of the director when I made my choices in how to approach that." Simcoe singles out the scene where he confronts Chiana and Jothee as both beautiful and difficult: "It was one of those occasions where we took a lot of time on the set before we started to shoot it, and it paid off. I loved working with Matt Newton."

Both Simcoe and Gigi Edgley wanted to ensure that the relationship between D'Argo and Chiana remained realistic. "We were really concerned about the diminuendo of that bond," he explains. "We didn't want them just to go on and be shipmates. We wanted reverberations of it to continue. There are moments in 'Dog with Two Bones' where you can still feel the echoes of the relationship. There's the echo of a sexual history between them, and that creates a really specific association that doesn't exist between D'Argo and the other characters. When you've been someone's lover, and you know them that well, even if you are not together any more, you can still push those buttons — you know what their vulnerabilities are, and what their strengths are. I think that both D'Argo and Chiana enjoy and exploit that knowledge of each other."

Simcoe is "really proud of the clear line of the relationship between D'Argo and Zhaan," and is hoping for something equally clear in his

dealings with the latest newcomer to Moya, Jool. "The writers are really trying to solidify that rapport," he says. "She needs to find some allies on the
ship, and I think that she is a really important trigger in D'Argo's development." Simcoe is pleased that this marks the end of what he refers to as the
"D'Argo as a petulant teenager" period: "We now need to find the new phase
of D'Argo, with him becoming a responsible adult — even if it's still a young,
impetuous one. Dealing with other 'children', like Chiana and Jool, has
been a great mechanism for showing that change."

It has helped tremendously that Simcoe and Tammy MacIntosh are old
friends. The scenes in '...Different Destinations' gave them a chance to
demonstrate how that could be a boon to the show. "It was great for us to
show our co-workers we know each other really well, and that we can spar
together really well!" Simcoe says. "If you are looking for some sort of comic
duo on *Farscape*, Tammy and I have such a long history together as mates
that we could improvise a lot of that stuff, with me throwing her over the
wall. It was great for me to get back into the groove with Tam."

On a more serious note, there have also been more of what David
Kemper termed the "Obi-Wan Kenobi" scenes between Crichton and
D'Argo, where the Luxan is a font of wisdom to his human friend. "That is
a direction we want to take," Simcoe affirms. "The writers were so impressed
with that scene between John and D'Argo in 'Look at the Princess'. Now I

think we're really seeing the full potential of D'Argo's intelligence come to the fore. Whereas before he was intelligent but immature, after his experiences with Crichton, his intelligence has been allowed to grow and blossom. I think you'll find a lot more of those 'Obi-Wan' moments, as he starts to distance himself a little bit, emotionally, from the other regulars, and look at life more objectively. I think that's going to make him wiser, and able to contribute more positively to the world of the characters on Moya."

That doesn't mean that Crichton and D'Argo will always see eye to eye. "Ben and I always wanted to explore more 'buddy stories'," Simcoe explains, pointing out that he and Ben Browder see the characters as resembling Butch Cassidy and the Sundance Kid from the classic Paul Newman/Robert Redford film. "There are elements of that in the episodes on Moya, but as D'Argo becomes older, you start to see the genuine challenge between the males fighting over who's going to make the decisions. That's more interesting for Crichton, and more interesting for D'Argo than just having Crichton as the definite leader. He ends up being that of course, because he is the audience's point of view for the show, but it's a more interesting path to that finality."

Most of the *Farscape* characters have had one major objective, which has become their overriding reason for staying together. But D'Argo has had several. "I feel really lucky that D'Argo has had a few super objectives," Simcoe says. "Each of those journeys has enabled me to reveal different things — whether it be dealing with Lo'Lann, or Jothee, or now coming back to the other angle of that problem and starting to think about Macton. I think that highlights the difference between where we started with D'Argo, and where we are now. Initially, he would have been hell-bent on killing, but now we start to see a real change in him, in that he wants to find justice. He's more interested in justice than revenge."

And having his very own spaceship definitely helps. "It's Cool Town!" Simcoe grins. "It's got a cloaking device and a big gun on the top of it, and I'm the only guy who can fly it — I love it! But seriously, D'Argo's new super objective is all tied up in that ship: it's become the centre of his whole presence on the show."

Looking back over his three seasons as D'Argo, Simcoe is delighted with his character's progress. "I think we've achieved softening D'Argo up and broadening him," he says. "Now we've just got to keep finding new ways to keep him fresh." ■

Chiana

" They always make it more complicated than what they need to. Use it against them. Screw them at their own game."

challenge is always good," says Gigi Edgley. "I like to eat them for breakfast!" That attitude certainly helped the actress during *Farscape*'s third year, when Chiana headed in directions that were very different to Edgley's expectations. "It's so tricky sometimes, because in your head you've established an emotional arc for your character, based on the rough plan that you are given," she admits. "But of course, that rough plan always gets changed, usually at the last minute!"

Season three certainly gave Edgley plenty of challenges. At the start of the year, the culmination of her fling with Jothee led to the young Luxan's departure from Moya, and the break up of D'Argo and Chiana's relationship. "I was very nervous about that," Edgley admits. "I think the writers were try-ing to get Chiana back to being that very non-trusting minx; kind of an Artful Dodger character. She was a Tinkerbell who has a bit of clang in her tink! There was a nice little bond between D'Argo and Chiana, but then all of a sudden it was blown out of the window as quickly as it appeared."

Edgley had numerous conversations with executive producer David Kemper about Chiana's decisions in 'Suns and Lovers': "I said to him, 'Hang on a minute: everything's going to hell, people are running around the ship screaming — and Chiana is getting down and dirty with tentacles and food? What's going on here?'"

The producer explained that they wanted to "spin Chiana on her heels" and keep the audience guessing as to what she was up to. "Doing that was really inviting, but also very frightening at the same time," Edgley says. "But it's what I endeavour to do — be bold with the choices." She was also glad that the relationship with D'Argo didn't disappear completely after 'Suns and Lovers'. "I was really excited about having some precious scenes with Crichton and D'Argo in 'Eat Me'," she explains. "It was really pleasing to explore the lingering relationship chemistry between D'Argo and Chiana, as there had been such an abrupt end to the partnership. It was lovely to play with the connection they had with each other. It's really helpful to Chiana's character when I'm given the opportunity to dive into such good writing, as I believe it helps show the audience that she has a heart too, although a lot of the time it seems very lost and confused."

Edgley says this is one of the keys to understanding Chiana through the season, even though she thinks that "it wasn't the season for Chiana to come to the fore. I know they wanted to strengthen the Crichton and Aeryn rela-tionship, and that was the focus. I believe Chiana's mistrusting heart is the

source of a lot of her problems, but she's learning all the time. In our every-day life, we are defined by our experiences, and we are a walking manifesta-tion of all that we learn along our journey. Each scene Chiana has lived through has made her all that she is. You get to learn just as much, if not more, standing in the background of the scene watching it all go by. It was nice to stand back for a while and see the ebb and flow of the show."

The actress also wanted to "put some of the 'chi' into Chiana. I was making really simple choices of her just watching, using her senses, and almost feeling people in the next room's breath on her skin. There were some really juicy episodes for Chiana though, and the ones that were nice and deep I loved. And she has managed to experience a lot of fun as well."

Edgley enjoyed the opportunity to demonstrate some new sides to Chiana, particularly with the firestick twirling in 'Scratch 'n' Sniff'. "I had mentioned to Tony Tilse that I wanted to find different, alien forms of attract-ing characters into Chiana's lair," she explains. "The scene in the nightclub was originally meant to involve a little of the usual, 'Hey, how you doin'?' vibe, with some girlie gyrating and giggling on the side. I became a little frus-trated that people believe these are the only tricks a girl has got up her sleeve, so later on Tony saw me fooling with the firesticks, and a few days later he had worked it into the script!"

'Revenging Angel' brought out a maternal side to Chiana that Edgley hadn't expected to see. "Much as I searched my soul and character, I just couldn't make it work," she admits. "Andrew Prowse explained that everyone else was slipping out of character so much that Chiana didn't realise she was becoming maternal."

Edgley found herself affected by her scenes in 'Dog with Two Bones' when she is burying Talyn's remains in the Leviathan burial ground. "It was a beautiful moment for Chiana, and for me," she says. "It reminded me of all the wonderful moments I've had living and breathing on Moya, and all the challenging ones as well. It reminded me of myself in the early days, and how nervous Chiana was being a midwife, bringing Talyn into the world. It conjured a beautiful feeling in my heart to remember how far I have come, and how far I have let Chiana emerge in my body, heart and soul."

Although Edgley is disappointed that Australian audiences are behind the rest of the world in the broadcasting of the series, she has found that the lack of immediate feedback has had advantages. "I think we've been very lucky in a way almost to have that protective bubble," she says. "You are a little bit more carefree: you're not so conscious of how it looks to the outside world. It's been good to remain a bit distant from what's coming out on the other side, to remain truthful just to your inner choice and to the other characters on set."

Portraying Chiana's journey has been a great experience for Edgley, who never misses a chance to continue to expand her character. "I endeavour to remember experiences within Chi's past history when I'm approaching each scene," she explains, "though at times it is very challenging, what with the work load and lack of sleep, to remind oneself of every detail of a character's life! Chiana is growing in a multitude of ways as the series continues. I really want to keep exploring her darker, dangerous side — the side that is searching for what life is all about. I want to quietly take her somewhere *very* different. I would love to fool around with the more bizarre aspects of the supernatural traits she's started showing...

"It's the most phenomenal blessing to be a part of this show," Edgley concludes. "The stories — the dreams and imaginings of our wonderful writers — live and breathe in the hearts of so many fans. I'm part of it all, and I want to make sure I surrender to the dream, just let go and use this amazing opportunity to its full extent!" ■

" Okay. I can do this. I can. I can do anything. That's what my father told me. That's what my mother told me, and I've never doubted them before."

"If I didn't have to play her, I would hate Jool!" Tammy MacIntosh admits. "But, not everyone in the world of *Farscape* is likeable, and that's just one of the things I loved about coming into this series."

The character of Joolushko Tunai Fenta Hovalis the Interion was deliberately introduced into the third season of *Farscape* to shake up the slightly cosy, domestic feel that the show might have started to exhibit without such a change. "I have a theory," explains MacIntosh, "that if actors stay and play too long in a television series, you start to get a situation where it's a bit too 'happy families'. You no longer have tension. Until, that is, you bring in new characters who can stir up the pot! New actors, who haven't had time to become too friendly with everyone, can really 'tear 'em to shreds' onscreen, without any personal upsets taking place off the set."

MacIntosh's audition process for *Farscape* took a long time, with the actress dedicating seven months to different tests, culminating in a final audition with Ben Browder — but at that stage she was not playing Jool. "The character I was given in the audition was very Aeryn-like," MacIntosh reveals. "Very military, very self-composed and very disciplined. There was a lot of sexual tension that had to be looked at between Ben and myself, and whether that would work. We ended up having a huge laugh, and played together very well. That was the point of the audition, so I got the job."

It was only then that MacIntosh discovered whom she would be portraying. Up to that point, "there was no hint of prosthetics, no hint of colour, no hint of costume — I had no idea who she was." The character ended up being partly inspired by MacIntosh herself, which the actress feels is another of the series' strengths: "David Kemper and the writers use a lot of you. They let you play, and then pick what they find most attractive, and what gets across to the audience. They don't try to turn your talents into something that they aren't."

The creation of Jool's look was also collaborative. "Dave Elsey said that there was a huge discussion about whether she should have blonde hair or red hair," MacIntosh recalls, "so I said to Andrew Prowse (who I've known for years), 'Why can't we have both? Why don't we say that when she gets angry, or there's an emotional moment, her blonde hair changes to red?' He thought that was a *great* idea!"

After all the prosthetics had been designed, MacIntosh discovered a major problem. "I had never worked with prosthetics before, and I really had no idea

how my skin would handle three hours in make-up, and eight layers of what I like to call 'house paint' — glues, chemicals and latex," she says. "It became quite apparent within the first three weeks that my skin was freaking out." Numerous tests followed to identify the particular chemical that was causing the reaction, after which MacIntosh's life became easier.

Playing the character also became easier as the season progressed. Initially, MacIntosh explains, "David Kemper had certain 'definites' about what he wanted to do with the character, but the rest he let me experiment with. He just told me to behave as if I'd been taken from the 'high life' and thrown into a shack in the outback of Western Australia, surrounded by cockroaches. All of a sudden, everything is just not right. She does *not* want to be there — it's not her world! I liked the fact that Jool was very hardcore, very bitchy and frankly, could be a real pain."

MacIntosh had the chance to paint further colours into the character in '...Different Destinations'. "They wrote this beautiful comedy stuff for me, and as soon as I hit that, it felt right," she recalls. 'Eat Me' allowed more development. "You got beyond the egotistical front that she'd put up," MacIntosh continues. "You actually got to encompass and feel her fear, and the child within her that is responsible for her behaviour."

With the discovery of an injured Crais, Jool stepped into Zhaan's shoes as the nearest thing that Moya has to a physician. "The only way she could survive

on that ship was to find something to do," MacIntosh says. "It's like coming from being a highborn princess and ending up in a grotty prison for the rest of your life. What are you going to do about that situation except either top yourself, or find something useful to do? It was nice to finally have that, because you can't have a character continue being that painful for too long, someone was going to shoot her! By that stage of the season, I was starting to get a bit frustrated with Jool's lack of emotional and intellectual growth on the ship, so the chance to bring that aspect to her character arrived at the right time."

MacIntosh enjoyed showing Jool going out of control on the pleasure planet in 'Scratch 'n' Sniff'. "For her, this was a brand new experience," she believes. "So I decided to play her like a child who has never done that sort of thing before, and see what happened. I think it made her fun for a change." The actress showed a more serious side of Jool in 'Revenging Angel'. "At that point she really needed a friend, because it was getting lonely, and everyone had just dissed her completely," she explains. "Jool revealed her heart and her soul, to some extent, to D'Argo, and it gave her a moment where you wanted finally to care about her. There hadn't been much for an audience to care about before that." She also enjoyed Jool's moment of glory. "It was nice to be wanted and needed — it's awful not to have any friends and be called a bitch the entire time!"

Her confrontation with Crais, at the start of 'I-Yensch, You-Yensch' after Talyn has destroyed the medical ship, was the wake-up call that MacIntosh feels Jool needed. "I don't think she has really opened her eyes to many of the things going on behind the scenes on Moya," she says. "Jool never really clicked on the history of these people, so it was good that she had the opportunity to lash out at Crais."

At the end of the year, Jool and the mysterious Old Woman are all who remain with Pilot aboard the Leviathan as it disappears into the wormhole, and MacIntosh is looking forward to what the new season will bring. "You can have everyone tough and gorgeous, or in love with Crichton, but that ain't the real world!" she points out. "You still need outside influences rocking the boat, to make that happy family not so happy. Then there's friction, and chaos — and those are opportunities for growth." ∎

> "I cannot bear to lose the one thing that mitigates the twisted core of my existence."

"Stark isn't a protagonist," Paul Goddard points out. "Generally, he's not the one to make things happen. Nor do things happen to him to create the drama. He's on the periphery." Goddard concedes that stories in the third year haven't exactly been built around the character of the former Banik slave. "There wasn't really a thought-out plan about how he was going to develop," he says. "I think Stark is a character who is written in such a way that he develops in the best way to serve the given situation." There are exceptions to every rule however, and it is Stark who precipitates events in '...Different Destinations', sending himself, Crichton, Aeryn, D'Argo and Jool back in time. "He's the time tunnel, basically," Goddard recalls.

At the start of the third season, Goddard was involved in some discussion with the producers regarding general ideas for Stark's progress during the year. "Some elements were mooted early on," he reveals. "There was no great conscious forethought about an emotional and character trajectory for him, but hints of the obsession with Aeryn were talked about very early on in the year. There were little hints of that, which came to a climax in 'The Choice' when she's on the planet looking for her father."

Goddard enjoyed laying the groundwork for Aeryn's emotional outburst at Stark — that he is "always watching" her. "How much of his interest in her is benign, and how much is malign you can't tell, because it's not there on screen," he explains. "Every now and again though, there were hints in previous episodes that it was a rather unhealthy obsession." Specifically, Goddard is referring to Stark's line to Aeryn that "you're very pretty" at the start of 'Eat Me', and "when he says, 'Thank you, thank you,' when they're on the planet with Crichton's dad in 'Infinite Possibilities'."

More than any other member of the crew, Stark is affected by Zhaan's death at the end of 'Wait for the Wheel'. "We didn't explore the calmer, spiritual side of him this season because of Zhaan's death," Goddard ventures. "Like everyone else, he was plunged into a rather chaotic, very fractured world, with the two spaceships going their separate ways."

Goddard acknowledges that there is also a very practical reason why Stark has not been seen in his calmer role, assisting other beings at their moment of death: "It costs an awful lot of money every time Stark takes his mask off!" he points out, referring to the extensive CG work needed to show Stark's glowing face. "In a sense, Stark's spiritual abilities have been put in a back drawer this season. We didn't get to see any extension of those, which

is his real area of expertise and power."

The actor tried hard not to overplay that other aspect of Stark's character — his madness and mania. "For me, it's tricky treading that fine line between being nauseatingly and gratuitously crazy, and being interestingly so," he says. "I always had a fear that there was a danger Stark's emotional and mental instability could become just a little annoying, in the way that they would in real life if you had somebody like that around. I'm sure that for some people, I didn't pull that off all of the time. I didn't want to be irritatingly zany. But some people find the craziness endearing!"

Goddard is also concerned about what other sides of Stark there are to portray, and enjoyed those moments when "his status was raised. I think that's why the comedy between him and Rygel worked. Their status on the ship is roughly equal, and though Rygel tries to lord it over Stark, there was a bit more of a battle of equals there in episodes like 'Green Eyed Monster', than when Rygel is battling with other crew members. They tend to put him down — as some of them do with Stark too."

'Meltdown' presented Goddard with "a fantastic opportunity for Stark to do something from out of left field again," he enthuses. "David Kemper

often talked about Stark being the kind of character where you simply don't know what he's going to do next. He can throw the whole ship into peril because of his instability and passions. 'Meltdown' was one instance where that was brought to the fore. Becoming Talyn's Pilot was a moment where his status was raised because he was powerful, and that was fabulous to play. I loved the power that he had — it showed all of his darker side."

Goddard also found an unexpected side effect from the scenes in 'The Choice' where Stark, Crais and Rygel are pinned down by the pulse fire from the Valdonnians. "I had the guns out and was firing away, and that was one of the easiest and most comfortable moments I've had actually," Goddard reveals. "Rowan Woods told me that I looked fantastic! It's so easy to feel the power of a character when they're pulling guns out and shooting people. As an actor, you feel different, too. After doing those scenes, I felt different on set, and more powerful as an actor."

The experience reminded him of his work on *The Matrix*, in which he played Agent Brown. "If you're wandering around with sunglasses on all day, and a gun in your holster, you really do feel sort of invincible as a person," he explains. "It's not identification with the character, though. You're role-playing, and you don't completely slip out of role at any time, especially when you're dressed in the clothes. When you're dressed as a clown, and you walk past a mirror, you feel like a clown when you see yourself. Playing Stark, who's put upon and insecure, you still have the slave mentality, and you feel as if you're still being treated a bit like a slave. And that's not as glamorous or as fun to play!"

Nevertheless, Goddard is always eager to read each new script for *Farscape*. "Right from the beginning, this show has always been about surprises, and throwing curveballs from left field and having fun," he enthuses. "I like to be thrown things that make me go, 'Wow, that was different!' Each time I get a script, I'm keen to see what the opportunities for my character are, and then go off and figure out something really interesting to do with them. I'm always looking for opportunities to have a laugh, and to have some dramatic moments. If I can do both in an episode, then that's great!" ■

" The last time I left this ship, my ship, I did so under a veil of secrecy... Well this time, Scorpius, I am not leaving quietly."

"I deliberately made the choice in the early days of the show not to reveal everything about him immediately," says Lani Tupu of his main *Farscape* persona, the former Peacekeeper captain Bialar Crais. Season three was filled with revelations however, leading up to the character's noble self-sacrifice at the end of 'Into the Lion's Den'.

"One thing about planning a long-running series is that there's always an effort not to give *everything* away in the first season," Tupu elaborates. "You're like a long distance runner. You have to pace yourself, you have to eke out what's known about the character and, in collaboration with the writers, keep the surprise element going all the way through, for years and years if necessary!"

Crais's strategic skills, his innate knowledge of the Command Carrier he once commanded, his bond with Talyn, his ability to bend people to his will and his love of honour — all combine with his belief in the validity of Crichton's cause to lead him inexorably to his destiny in season three. "It's a wonderful, selfless act on his part," Tupu believes, "although not so selfless in a way, because he is also protecting Talyn. Ultimately, there is only one way to get out of the predicament with regards to Scorpius — and he *hates* Scorpius!"

Tupu thinks that Crais had the scheme to destroy the Command Carrier in the back of his mind much earlier than he lets on. "I think that to a degree it was absolutely predetermined," he says. "I figured that Crais had actually thought this through carefully, and he knew exactly how to get on the Command Carrier. The only way he could get close to Scorpius was by offering Talyn as a sacrificial lamb. No one else could have done it, and he knows that for once in his life he's actually made one massive decision that will have major repercussions down the track. For that very reason I think he's at peace with himself at that moment of destruction. I have this idea that Crais had to go full circle. He started out on the track of revenge, but then came back full circle to a major understanding, either about himself or the people that he's involved with, and then he reached completion."

However, not everything about Crais is noble during the third year. An important theme, as Tupu sees it, is Crais's need to be in control. That is partly why he welcomes the opportunity to be a teacher to the young gunship, Talyn, and then to have former subordinate Aeryn Sun aboard. When Talyn's crew are affected by the drexin gas in 'Meltdown', Crais becomes "almost Mussolini-ish" in his behaviour. "There's this wonderful moment where he tries to hammer down the door," Tupu recalls, "and you know by that stage Crais has just completely lost it, because there is no way that he's

going to actually break down the door. He's screaming at Talyn, and then he turns round and screams at Aeryn — and she just looks at him and walks away. That was a great comic moment, because I pushed it to the limit, he's completely irrational. The interesting thing about Crais is that when he's in control, he's very cool, calm and collected. Even though he's passionate, he knows exactly what he's doing and he's very clear about his agenda. He's never irrational — that's why it's so effective in 'Meltdown' when he does flip. I loved playing those moments, where he screams at everybody!"

It is the moment when he realises he cannot control Crichton and Aeryn that pushes Crais over the edge, Tupu believes. "He actually wants to get some very important business done," the actor recalls, "and he looks at them, and sees what's happening between them. That's when it really gets underneath his skin. He's really never had the chance to be jealous before."

With neither Stark nor Rygel prepared to act under his command, that only leaves Talyn, so Crais tries to continue his tutelage of the young gunship. "Crais needs to be in control," Tupu confirms, "and his whole thing with Talyn was wanting to be able to control this powerful ship. He can't control Aeryn, and he's *never* going to be able to control Crichton… Talyn was the only element that he could possibly have power over, but then it

turns out that there's no way he can control him either!" As the gunship grows, he becomes able to inflict pain on Crais, both physically and mentally. "I think the relationship with Talyn has caused Crais a lot of soul searching," Tupu says. "There's a wonderful handful of scenes where I'm going crazy on the ship, and it's Talyn's doing."

The relationship between Crais and Talyn is altered by Aeryn's presence on board. Talyn's attitude to Aeryn is at times unhealthy, although, as Tupu points out, "she's like a mother figure to him. She was the only one who initially understood who Talyn was, or at least had an insight into who he possibly was. At first Crais was rigidly military in his approach to Talyn. He is a brilliant strategist, and he teaches Talyn strategy, but there was no room for emotion. That ended up becoming one of the wonderful aspects of this Talyn/Crais relationship, but it was brought out by Aeryn. She brings in the ability to feel, and the ability to be vulnerable."

Once on board the Command Carrier, Crais is reunited with Darinta Narrell, his former lover who has been put through the Aurora Chair since Crais's defection. Tupu relished the opportunity to play some romantic scenes — as he did any scene that displayed a new side to the Peacekeeper captain. "One of the things I love about Crais, which has always been at the forefront of my thinking about him, is that he can really surprise you," he explains. "What I enjoy about playing this character is that, even though as an actor I know what's coming up (I've read the scripts, you see!), I have chosen not to give anything away, not show anything on screen, until it happens. And then — 'Bam!' That's one of the best moments that you can have as an actor, and it certainly makes it much more interesting for an audience. If the audience is tipped off in advance by something in your performance, then there's no element of surprise, and therefore no mystery. Keeping a sense of mystery is one of the most powerful tools an actor has with a character. If everything is a foregone conclusion to the viewer, you may as well pack up your bags and go home!

"*Farscape* as a whole is certainly still keeping that element of surprise and mystery," Tupu concludes. "This is the fourth year coming up, and the audience are still hanging in there! I think that's a wonderful testament to everybody working on the show." ■

" You think I want wormholes to betray Peacekeepers and to conquer the universe myself? I don't want power. I want *revenge*."

"I moved Scorpy a long way in year three," says Wayne Pygram. "He's certainly become more passionate, and has revealed a little bit more of himself. I'm pretty happy with it all." Pygram has effectively had three roles during the season — as the neural clone of Scorpius inside the heads of both John Crichtons, and as the wormhole-obsessed Scarran-Sebacean hybrid himself. He even had the opportunity, in 'Incubator', to show Scorpius as he was in his formative years.

Although Pygram didn't play the infant hybrid, he was inside the more unsightly prosthetic that adorned the teenage Scorpius. "I like to think that I showed his innocence, his willingness to succeed, and his belief in himself," he comments. "He took a risk, laying himself on the line like that, presenting himself to the Peacekeepers and surrendering. They could have just marched him outside and got rid of him, so it was a big gamble. It was wonderful to see this young man with such energy and clarity of purpose. He has a steeliness about him, and an absolute, unconditional self-belief. You knew that even if the Peacekeepers had said no to him and thrown him out, he would have found some other way of moving forward and establishing himself as an entity to be reckoned with. He was always going to be successful somewhere, somehow. Ironically, the things that made him such a freak are the things that are of value to him, and to others. His mission, in a funny way, is to be valuable to others — he is of extreme value, but they just don't get it. The way he looks doesn't give people much confidence, but he wins that confidence very quickly once he looks them in the eye. He's so sure of himself, it's almost unnerving.

"As he gets older, things begin to get a bit clouded," Pygram adds. "Scorpy starts to play politics. He's learning how to play the game. He's happy to present himself as totally, one hundred per cent committed to a project, or to the Peacekeepers, but he's developed some other agendas along the way..." Some of that game-playing seems to have come back to haunt him in 'Lambs to the Slaughter', when Scorpius is carpeted by Commandant Grayza. "There's some connection between them," Pygram believes. "Maybe Scorpius has trod on her toes, undermined her or somehow embarrassed her. There's more to her than meets the eye."

The actor wonders why Scorpius keeps Lieutenant Braca around. "He does screw up," he laughs. "But he would die for Scorpius — he's a very loyal foot servant. I suspect that Scorpius has faith that Braca isn't going to sell him out. But I think there's an opportunity for a revelation about Braca —

he's literally on a leash, so maybe Scorpy's put a neural chip inside him! He might be more useful than we think."

Pygram is pleased with Scorpius's development through the year. "He's more openly emotional," he points out. "He has become more vulnerable, which makes him perhaps a little less 'alien', so he's got closer to Crichton in lots of ways. And Crichton is far more confident in the way he deals with Scorpius. He's not fearful at all. He has a certain knowledge of Scorpius now, and can predict how he's going to react."

Although Scorpius is obsessed with cracking the secret of wormholes, Pygram doesn't think that it's the 'be all and end all' for him. "When it comes to the crunch, he has other things to attend to," he explains. "He's got his Command Carrier collapsing around him, and he has to deal with that. It shows that he's not totally desperate — he can wait for his piece of pie. But he has now become a loose cannon. I don't think that diminishes him — I was worried that it would, showing his overwhelming passion — but you've got to go somewhere with the character, and if you are going to get really passionate, it might as well be about something as big as control of the universe! So I thought it was appropriate. Scorpius went on a bit of a journey this season," he concludes. "I've had to take him somewhere else, but I know I'm in good hands."

Pygram's other role is the neural clone, dubbed Harvey (after the classic James Stewart film) by Crichton. "I'm lucky in that I've been given another character to do something different with," the actor says. "There's always a risk that if you experiment with a character too much, you can stitch yourself up, and undermine what you've established. I'd like to think I'll never go down that road with Scorpius, because I get the chance to look for fresh, new things in this other character — the clone. I see him as a real opportunity for me as an actor, and for the series as well, because those scenes allow for a totally different rhythm and feel to the rest of the show. I loved all that allegorical stuff. I loved all the World War Two bits, playing chequers and cards with Crichton. The clone is a storyline inside a storyline inside a storyline — it's like one of those Russian dolls."

The sense of inquisitiveness that the clone has demonstrated has pleased Pygram. "It's been a season of deliberation for the clone," he says. "It's a good structural device to use him as a sounding board for Crichton, and it's written with some tightness, with the clone actually fuelling the main story. He's becoming a window to, or a mirror for, the main narrative, which means it's not just a nice, quirky idea, but an important part of the whole. He becomes somewhere for Crichton to retreat to — the clone can't really give a clear answer, but he can point Crichton in the right direction. He can get him to reassess things."

Playing the clone has given Pygram numerous unusual opportunities and he has relished them all. "All the days playing the Scorpy clone are memorable," he maintains, "whether it's the undertaker in 'Revenging Angel', or the day at Luna Park filming the dodgems and the rollercoaster ride. They are all like little cameos, and every day was fantastic. It gives me the chance to have some fun, particularly in episodes where I had to dress up. I'd be laughing at myself — and I always figure that's a bit of a plus when you're at work."

Looking ahead to season four, Pygram says that "the biggest interest I can create is one of surprise. I feel confident to move forward with the clone, and hopefully stretch it even further. There is obviously no confusion about the two separate characters — the impact of the real Scorpius is not lessened in any way by having this loony version running around inside Crichton's brain, so hopefully there will be even more zany opportunities for me to explore!" ∎

"Mother always said I'd die from incompetence. I finally know what she meant."

hen David Kemper and I first discussed Rygel, we talked about him, funnily enough, as Hamlet," voice artist Jonathan Hardy recalls. "He's a character who is really defined by the people around him, rather than being positively one thing in his own right."

During the third season of *Farscape*, the events and other characters Rygel found himself amongst gave the Hynerian a chance to demonstrate numerous facets — a besotted lover in 'Fractures', and a crafty diplomat in 'Thanks for Sharing' and 'I-Yensch, You-Yensch' for example, as well as what Hardy describes as "an heroic little battler" in 'Infinite Possibilities'. Tim Mieville, head of the puppetry team operating Rygel, points out that "you can't do any one aspect of Rygel all the time, you have to broaden the character a bit. His nasty moments are lovely to do when they come up, though!"

"It always astonishes me when people say that Rygel's nasty, and a scumbag," Hardy says. "I still maintain that Rygel has more inherent dramatic nobility than most of the others. Rygel can be self-centred when he is required to be self-centred, but he also has extreme cunning and political savvy. He can also be quite kindly, like when he said goodbye to Zhaan, which was an almost tear-jerking moment, or when he said goodbye to the other Crichton. A lot of people do find him a fascinating character."

Mieville agrees. "The writers are careful to come up with some really good moments for Rygel," he notes. "If you make him too selfish, then eventually people get bored. During the third season he was giving advice to Crichton at one stage, and to Aeryn. Crichton has learned over the cycles that Rygel has his place and his worth. He was treated as an equal in Crichton's death scene and not just as someone in the background. He comes forward and does his bit."

The writers have also fleshed out more of the Dominar's backstory, with the revelation of the Hynerians' hatred of the Charrids. Mieville relished the scene where Rygel takes his revenge on the Charrid prisoner. "He doesn't think twice about torturing him. Then he had a great time in those episodes blasting away at his mortal enemies!" he recalls. "I really like it when he's at his most heroic, because you suddenly see that the little guy has some fibre," Hardy adds. "It's like living with a chihuahua. You think it's this little squeaking thing, and suddenly it goes and savages an intruder, and you realise, 'Oh, there was something to that chihuahua after all!' I don't think that Rygel should just be a comic character — he has real breadth."

The veteran actor sees Rygel "as, strangely, one of the most 'human' of

the crew. He doesn't have the strength that other people have, but he does have that desperate need to protect himself, and the need to hope for the future. I think a lot of people who are battlers have the same thing. He's not actually equipped with anything to get him on in the humanoid world, and yet in reflecting certain human values, he comments on the human race.

"His central core is that he can respond to anything," Hardy offers. "Some of the speeches that he makes are quite Shakespearean in their own way, and certainly quite heroic, and I think it's that aspect of his character which makes him most appealing. When the pressure's on, Rygel's going to react. Now it may well be in a way that suits him most, rather than the group, but when it comes down to it, how many people *do* fight for the group? That seems to me something that is an aspiration rather than a fact. But Rygel ends up doing good things for people despite himself, as a by-product of his way, which I find quaintly Buddhist!"

In contrast, Mieville admits that "I really love those little moments when Rygel's a bit of a wuss. He can be like a little child. One of the first lines he's got in *Farscape* is, 'Mother thinks I looked the best.' He's got a mother complex: there are moments where we can almost see the teddy bear under his arm! I love those touches because they pop up so rarely amongst the humorous and the savage moments, or the selfish ones."

Another aspect of Rygel explored in season three was his love life, touched upon in 'The Choice'. "One of the soothsayers reveals a little bit about a past girlfriend," Mieville recalls. "That was a lovely scene, because there he was being entirely dismissive of the whole experience, and then suddenly he's not pooh-poohing it any more!"

When Rygel returns to Moya, he discovers that a female Hynerian is on board, and for the rest of 'Fractures', he becomes blind to her faults — until far too late. "Well, I didn't like her at all," Hardy jokes. "But then, if you'd been at sea for 300 years or whatever, you'd go for anything! I'm a bit confused about Rygel sometimes, because he did say at one point to Zhaan that he's not really a 'body breeder'. But then again, he did try once with Chiana in a barrel!"

Rygel has had his comic moments throughout the season, notably where he is paired with Stark. Even though Hardy is not on set with Paul Goddard, the two men "are fairly heavily into the classics as actors, so we're on the same wavelength, in a way," Hardy explains. "We do know each other, and though we may never actually act together in the same room, we each understand how the other will approach a scene. I especially like the verbal gymnastics between our characters!"

In 'I-Yensch, You-Yensch', Rygel enters into a pragmatic relationship with Scorpius against a common foe. "They swapped ideas, they swapped respect," Mieville points out. "There was a symbolic scene at the end that was very powerful, I thought." Hardy agrees: "I think that was astonishing because they're two very extreme characters who can find in that extremeness, as it were, a fellow feeling. They speak very clearly to one another. Better the devil you know, I suppose."

Scorpius provides Rygel with the news that Dominar Bishan's reign is in trouble, which gives him a reason to leave Moya. "Rygel had a very dark patch for a couple of seasons, because he didn't know what his future would be if he went home," Mieville says. "But now he realises that there is a future for him, so he does actually want to get back."

Hardy looks forward to the new twists and turns in the Dominar's life. "I'm of the school of acting that says you are there to serve the writers," he says, "but you can only serve the writers inasmuch as they give you things to serve them with. Hopefully what we've seen of Rygel in the third year will help them to continue to develop the character. He's not just a little clown, or an evil little menace, or a self-centred anything. He's a hero! But then, I would say that." ∎

" I understand, Crichton. However, my inclination is not to accept any explanation."

F or Lani Tupu, one of the biggest changes about playing Pilot for the third season was that the character, previously so subservient, was now beginning to voice his opinions. Tupu had considered that the series should capitalise on the facets of the character that were first displayed in season two's 'The Way We Weren't'. "That episode showed me the direction I thought he should be taking. In the flashbacks, we saw the young Pilot actually having an opinion and a voice about what he wanted to do — but that wasn't echoed in many episodes after that," he points out. "I thought that was a lost opportunity. We'd heard his interior thoughts and feelings, but then through the rest of that season we didn't really hear anything more about what he was thinking. It's crucial when you're voicing a character that they have an opinion. Once they have an opinion, you can empathise with them. I get a real sense of who the characters are in *Shrek*, for example, because they all have their own views about things.

"When I'm in the ADR room dubbing his voice, I don't concentrate on Pilot's visage or his exterior — I'm always focusing on his emotions and his feelings," Tupu adds. "That was the difficulty: if you didn't play emotions with Pilot, what he said just ended up being a series of commands, and that didn't satisfy me, or the audience. If the audience don't have an emotional connection with a character, then they aren't following the story in its truest sense."

The change in the character was first seen in the third year's opening episode. "When Pilot snaps at Chiana and Jothee in 'Season of Death', I knew from that moment on that we couldn't just have Pilot being on the sidelines, with nothing to say," Tupu maintains. "I remember going in to ADR, and thinking that if he was having a go at these two, he should be having an opinion about other things as well. After all, he sees everything that's happening on the ship, but he hadn't been given a real voice, other than just being a pilot, and making sure that everybody got safely from A to B without too much trouble. Pilot having his own views gave me more room to move as an actor, and I didn't feel so confined."

Tupu feels that Zhaan's death robs Pilot of "somebody he can have an empathy with. He doesn't have Zhaan any more, and the frustration of seeing everybody else on board making their mistakes must have an effect on him. It's great to see him turn and let them know exactly what he thinks of them." A good example of this comes in 'Scratch 'n' Sniff': "Crichton and D'Argo learn that there is now a boundary they just can't push with Pilot," Tupu points out. "When they go down to the Pleasure Planet and get

absolutely smashed, he just rips into them, and that was a wonderful moment to play. He's not just giving or taking commands in his role as Pilot — he's really telling them what he thinks of them!"

Tupu enjoyed the wide range of vocal expression that the third season gave him as Pilot, particularly when he is possessed in 'Losing Time'. "That was wild. I had to twist my head round, and think about him from another angle," the actor explains. "I had to be a completely different character within Pilot's body — as if it wasn't schizophrenic enough already, what with me and all the puppeteers! I see what's on the screen and I work within what the puppetry team have given me," Tupu continues. "When I'm working, I close my eyes at various points and just work on the emotion at the time it's needed, especially when Pilot is screaming or is in pain. I can be screaming for about fifteen minutes, which is great fun! Sometimes."

While Pilot is beginning to express more of his own opinions, Moya is his primary concern, and he continues to act as the conduit through which she communicates her feelings to the crew. He has indicated that the Leviathan enjoys the crew's company — at least when they're not all at each other's throats. And even if Pilot is not in a position to act as her intermediary, Moya finds a way of communicating with and assisting them — as when she helps Crichton get rid of the rider who infests Pilot in 'Losing Time', by using one of the DRDs. Nevertheless, Pilot does admit in 'Incubator' that both he and Moya would relish the opportunity for exploration that travelling through the reaches

of deep space with the Relgarian Linfer would bring, and later, when Crichton plans to attack the Command Carrier, Moya is not a willing participant. She stays in hiding while the crew board Scorpius's ship, admitting, via Pilot, that she would rather die than submit to a control collar once more.

Moya has priorities of her own, and through the third season, we see the Leviathan demonstrating her love for her errant son, Talyn. In 'Eat Me' she StarBursts without warning when she hears his distress call, abandoning Crichton, D'Argo, Chiana and Jool in a transport pod. In 'Thanks for Sharing', she refuses to leave Talyn while he is still recuperating. However, when Talyn has no option except to leave her at the end of that episode, Moya settles back down to peaceful co-operation with those who remain on board.

Her maternal instincts are put to the test once again when Talyn returns to Moya's side in 'Fractures'. When he destroys an innocent medical vessel and then turns and attacks Moya herself, the Leviathan reluctantly agrees that he needs help. Then, after Talyn's noble death on board the Command Carrier, Moya insists that the gunship's remains must be laid to rest in the Kelsa Yon, an ancient Leviathan burial ground. When she encounters a rogue Leviathan who seems intent on stopping her from achieving her wishes, she has no hesitation in asking the crew to kill it.

Lani Tupu feels that the decision was a pragmatic one, forced on Pilot and Moya by the situation. "They understood that there was no other choice," he reasons. "I keep reminding myself that in the depths of space, there are actually very few choices that one can make for survival. It's quick thinking that will save the day, even if it goes against your own feelings. You can be blown up in a millisecond, and that forces characters to make snap decisions which sometime later on they might sit down, chew over, and regret. I thought of it in terms of euthanasia — the rogue Leviathan is ill, it is endangering everyone else, and it just has to go. It's a harsh decision Pilot and Moya make, but it had to be made, nevertheless. It certainly makes you realise that Pilot and Moya aren't always 'nice'! Having compassion doesn't always mean that to keep something alive is the best choice."

Tupu hopes that Pilot might become a stabilising influence on the crew. "I think we've gone through three seasons where we've learned that all of the crew have got their own individual strengths," he says, "but they really would not survive without each other. What tends to happen with a group of people in a high-pressure situation is that it brings out the best in some, but the worst in others. So everything is constantly fluctuating — and they will need this creature who can deal with them all on an equal basis." ■

David Kemper

> "We've been fortunate enough to have many great Australian actors, on their way to and from Hollywood, stop and play in our sandbox for a while."

"The writers provided a never-ending amount of exquisite lunacy for me to throw myself into, and to be honest, the more eccentric they made **Zhaan**, the better it was for me," recalls Virginia Hey.

Zhaan's journey with the crew of Moya finally came to an end when she died to save the others at the climax of 'Self-Inflicted Wounds'. However, Hey feels that her sacrifice actually occurred earlier, "saving Aeryn in 'Season of Death'. Really, it came at that point, even before she finally made the grand sacrifice by manning that ship which was going to disintegrate. Of course, she knew that she was already dying. Originally the crew's plan had been to plant Zhaan. All the way through 'Suns and Lovers' and into 'Self-Inflicted Wounds', there was mention of finding a planet for Zhaan, and lots of discussion of leaving her there to recuperate. It's amazing that she didn't take Crichton aside at the start of 'Self-Inflicted Wounds' and say, 'Darling, wait for the wormhole, would you? Just pop me down on the planet first, and then you can go off chasing it!' But she didn't, and with Crichton chasing the wormhole, Zhaan lost her opportunity to be planted, and to be saved."

Zhaan

> "There is no guilt. There is no blame. There is only what was meant to be."

When the time came for Zhaan to make her choice, Hey was not surprised that the Delvian acted as she did. "One couldn't imagine any other kind of death for her," she points out. "She's an incredibly giving, beautiful soul, so it's no surprise that she would sacrifice herself. This is just supposition, but even if she had been able-bodied, she would *still* have sacrificed herself to save her 'family'. She was very much in love with all of them."

Hey found herself very affected by Zhaan's farewell. "The writers have such genius that I'm constantly surprised at every word that they write, because of the magic and wonder of it all," she says. "David Kemper wrote the most exquisite script. It was very beautiful, and extremely religious. It was very hard for me as an actress, as well as a character, to say goodbye to everybody in that way, and have that closure with everyone. The most moving for me was with Aeryn — it was extraordinary. Usually Aeryn doesn't show much emotion, so for Aeryn to envelop me in emotion really meant a lot to me. And in doing so, of course, Claudia did as well, so that was very special. It was sad for me to lessen my involvement with all those wonderful people that I had shared my time with. It was a sad, difficult time for me as Zhaan, but also for me as Virginia — when the director calls action, I feel that we are one and the same!"

"She was the mother from hell," says Linda Cropper of **Xhalax Sun**. Cropper had previously appeared as one of the Plokavians in season two's 'The Ugly Truth', and returned to portray "an incredibly strong warrior. I knew that she had to have strength, and the commando element to her, but that she had layers of pain beneath that. It was stressed to me that this wasn't just a one-dimensional role — she may be the 'mother from hell in outer space', but she's got a past. The producers told me it was a good, interesting part, a multi-faceted character. And they were right — it was great fun to play her!"

Cropper was surprised to find that the make-up process took some time. "It was just that rather large scar down one side of my face," she remembers, "and I thought it was going to take a lot less time to apply than the Plokavian make-up. Ironically enough, it actually took a lot longer this time around. The Plokavian make-up covered the whole head, so it was like putting on a bathing cap. Because this one had all that fine scar work around the eye, it took a long time to get on and off. I did like the fact she had a particularly vicious war wound though."

The actress enjoyed the challenges that playing Xhalax Sun brought. "I'm not normally an army commando type," she laughs. "I've played the odd criminal, and done a bit of gun fighting before, but not a lot of fist fighting. When you're in the moment, it's great to think that you are a total bitch, you've got a huge pulse rifle, and you're going to shoot the hell out of whoever comes around the corner!"

Xhalax

"I died a long time ago, Aeryn. You live for me."

Cropper relished Xhalax's death scene. "We spent a lot of time with Rowan Woods talking about Aeryn's father, and getting the timeframe right and the story really clear, but ultimately it was a scene between Aeryn and her mother. I thought that setting it all on a window ledge, and for them to be trying to make their peace in a bizarre kind of way, was really appropriate. It was noble but not soft." Cropper saw Xhalax's ultimate choice as her only course of action. "She had to do what was honourable," she points out. "She knew what she had been, she knew she deserved to die. She had that warrior honour."

"When I first started the show, I felt like Lieutenant Exposition," admits David Franklin, who plays **Braca**. "I was a device for Scorpius: someone for him to explain the plot to. But this season, it's been a gradual process of becoming a genuine player, being one of the links in the show. Braca has a past, a present — and a precarious future!"

Franklin doesn't think that Braca shares Scorpius's obsession with obtaining the wormhole technology from Crichton, although he does understand that it can bring great power — and possibly the saving of the Sebacean race. "The wormholes aren't his passion," Franklin confirms. "Survival and power are his passions — with survival first. Braca's been tap dancing really well. He's managed very quietly to insinuate himself into the lives of very important people, and make them need him. I think Scorpius has actually started to need Braca and lean on him, which I think Scorpius would never intentionally do. After all, how many people could one completely trust with one's life?"

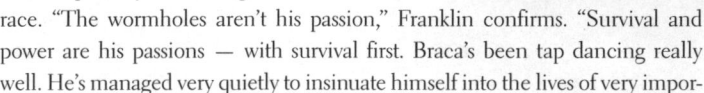

Braca

" I hope my conduct continues to find favour."

The actor enjoyed Braca's brief scene with Crais on the Command Carrier, when the former Peacekeeper captain reveals that he had expected Braca to continue to rise. "And there's still further that Braca can go," Franklin adds. "Power is such an aphrodisiac. He's managed to keep reasonably sober, otherwise he would have a klennan rod shoved right up his clacker! He's certainly coming into his own. So far, he's picked a winner with Scorpius, so he's able to relax a little more — even though you can never completely relax with Scorpius. That would be a fateful error! He's had a little bit more leeway to come out of his shell. That's been good for him — but I don't know about anyone else."

Franklin has also enjoyed being more heavily involved with the series. "Wayne's really good to work with," he says. "He'll come in and have really strong ideas, but he's also more than happy to try new things, to play about a bit." The actor has a gleam in his eye when he thinks about Braca's future now that Scorpius has lost his Command Carrier. "It'll be interesting to see what happens if Braca actually gets power," he says. "It could a case of being careful what you wish for — that could be his Achilles' heel!" ∎

THE EFFECTS

" Godlike aliens. Boy, do I hate godlike aliens. I'll take a critter over a

godlike alien any time..."

– John Crichton

THE CREATURE SHOP

"The Creature Shop and the puppeteers are the unsung heroes on *Farscape*. Their work just keeps getting better and better."

e never know what we are getting into until we get back to the studio at Homebush at the start of pre-production," Sydney Creature Shop creative supervisor Dave Elsey reveals. "For season three, we came in fairly open-minded and just ploughed straight into it!"

Taking back their workspace after the BBC had used it for their Olympic Games coverage during *Farscape*'s hiatus, Elsey and his crew made some structural changes: building an upper level which housed Elsey's office, a comfortable waiting area and offices for Sean Masterson and the puppeteers. They were all going to need the extra space as the demands of the third season grew.

As pre-production began, Elsey once again reviewed the make-ups for the regular characters. "Since season one, we've been trying to make Rygel better and better," he explains, "and I think in the third season he looked the best he's ever looked. We really got the skins and the seaming worked out, and we improved his hair. It fitted his character as this vain, preening emperor."

Although neither D'Argo nor Pilot required any major work to be done, Elsey and his team continued in their efforts to make Scorpius's make-up more comfortable for Wayne Pygram. "Unless you've ever been in make-up for any period of time, it's hard to know what the problems are, and how mad you go," Elsey says. "It's very difficult, and actors can really get an aversion to it. It's weird — you can't touch your face, you can't do any of the normal things. You can't lie down or get comfortable."

The biggest change was to Zhaan. As Virginia Hey had grown her hair between seasons, and was not cutting it off for the four episodes that she was appearing in, "we had to make her bald again." Elsey says. "We sculpted a foam latex bald-cap for her, and handed that over to the make-up department to actually do the fitting. We had to do that, because there are so many prosthetic characters on the show, and still only the same amount of prosthetic people who can actually stick things on, so we share a lot more with the make-up department than we used to."

'Season of Death' saw the unexpected return of the Diagnosan, Tocot, whom everyone thought had been killed at the end of 'Die Me, Dichotomy'. "We still had the costume," Elsey recalls, "but his breathing mask didn't exist any more. That gave us the opportunity to come up with a new design, because we knew he was going to be basically burned in his death scene, although there would be an optical effect over the top to dis-

guise it. We wanted to have as much of his face showing as we possibly could, so we came up with the idea that he would have a bunch of these masks stored all the way around the facility, since his life depended on them. So he could grab a new, clear mask. We also built an effects head for his death scene," Elsey adds. "It isn't really seen because of the opticals over the top, but it had air bladders, and smoke that came out, with bubbling features!"

Once again, Thomas Holesgrove played Tocot, and continued to be a stalwart inhabitant of Elsey's designs throughout the third year. "It really does make a difference having Thomas in the suits," Elsey smiles. "He keeps the whole thing alive — he makes sure that everything breathes, you can actually see the chest rising and falling as it were."

For 'Season of Death', Holesgrove also played Plonek, the Scarran who kills Tocot. Each time the Scarrans have been seen on *Farscape* there have been subtle differences in their appearance. "When we built the first Scarran in season two, we didn't know that we were ever going to see another one again, so it was kind of thrown together," Elsey admits, "but now every time we rebuild it, we update and refine it. We had a torturer Scarran in 'Won't Get Fooled Again', and an army Scarran in 'Season of Death'. The Scarran race isn't like the Daleks or the Cybermen from *Doctor Who*, who basically all look the same. We want to have a whole society of Scarrans, where they are all different, like people on Earth are all different. We created the female Scarran for 'Incubator', and they are smaller and sleeker — different, yet still very Scarran. The pirate Scarran, Naj Gill, in 'Fractures' has a sleeker look too."

Although Terry Ryan continues to design the clothing for the cast, as *Farscape* has progressed, a balance has been reached between the costume department and the Creature Shop, which means that Lou Elsey creates many of the costumes for the prosthetic and animatronic creatures. "It's usually a joint discussion between Dave and myself," Lou Elsey explains. "He comes up with the idea he wants, and I have to take into account that they have to be functional. You have to hide seams and be able to get the actor in and out of the costume very quickly. Everything is hugely character-based. I like to bring in a bit more detail, and not make it look as if they are just wearing clothes. It should look like it's something from their heritage, rather than an alien wearing a frock! With the pirate Scarran, we thought that he would have stolen a lot of his costume, and worn it as a trophy — we had loads of different aspects that nevertheless went together and had a harmonious feel. That was really nice to get my teeth into — I could go a little bit mad with that one!"

Dave Elsey brought his past experience working on horror films to bear on a number of the creatures in *Farscape*'s third year, and was also responsible for Grunchlk's memorable finger-biting scene in 'Season of Death'. "I thought that was more horrible because we *didn't* use red blood," Elsey observes. "We did not want red to come out, because he's not human. We tried to think of another colour, and someone suggested pink, because that wouldn't be offensive. And for some reason the pink blood that comes out of his finger and dribbles down his chin is the most offensive thing I've ever seen in my life!"

'Eat Me', another horrific episode, gave Elsey the chance to work with one of his idols. Although originally Kaarvok was going to be created as half make-up and half animatronic, rewrites of the script meant that the character became "more of an Anthony Hopkins type of role" — the charm of Hannibal Lecter combined with the horror of his deeds. "I didn't have any idea of what Kaarvok would look like, and they cast this charming English guy, who turned up at the workshop for his lifecast," Elsey recalls. "As soon as I saw him, I realised that I knew his face — I recognised his eyebrows! As a kid, there was nothing I wanted to be more than Baron Frankenstein, or at the very least his assistant, so I was delighted to find myself working with Shane Briant, who of course had starred with Peter Cushing as the Baron, in the movie *Frankenstein and the Monster from Hell.*"

Chatting with Briant about the various Hammer horror films in which he had appeared inspired Elsey, who took his ideas to the writers and producers. "We came up with the idea that Kaarvok had probably undergone some kind of hideous brain operation at some point, and had a metal plate put in, which he's been picking at," he explains. "The skin's started to flake away, and he's exposed a huge lump of his head — it

Page 137: Thomas Holesgrove unmasked.

Opposite page: Design art for the female Scarran.

Above: How she ultimately appeared, in 'Incubator'.

showed how mad and decayed the whole thing had become."

Inspiration continued to strike even as the filming began. "We had brilliant times in the make-up chair talking about the Hammer films Shane had done, and we also mentioned the Vincent Price movie *The Abominable Dr. Phibes*," Elsey says. "Phibes has a thing in his neck that he speaks through, and somehow he drinks a glass of champagne through the back of his neck! You never figure out how, but you hear him gulping. So we had the idea of a tube that shoots out of Kaarvok's arm, which goes into his victim's brain, liquefies it and sucks it up into the tube. I said to Shane that he should just stick the tube in his ear and inject the brain fluid into his head. Ian Watson, the director, thought it was a great image and totally went with it — although he took out the gulping, because that really did take it over the edge!"

The creation of Jool was another example of the discussion process operating on *Farscape*. "Normally what happens is that we'll get a script, I'll say what I think the character should look like, they say that's great, and David Kemper adjusts it and writes down a few things that fit with the design," Elsey explains. "With Jool, it was much more important to get the character right. They very much wanted it to be the actress's own face — they wanted minimal prosthetics, because they didn't want it to be a nightmare making her up every day. I tried to explain that sometimes it's better to go *more* alien, because that way you can actually do a quicker make-up. However, they were hiring the actress for her face, and they were really concerned that we didn't cover her up."

There were other considerations that Elsey had to take into account. "David told me that a joule was a scientific term for heat, and that was what Jool was meant to supply to the show — she was going to upset people and cause arguments. I also think it's really important to create an iconographic look for the characters — if you see a picture of one of the aliens on the show, especially Zhaan or Scorpius, you can tell it's *Farscape* from across the room. So I really wanted red hair, and a flame motif for the front of her hair, which would tie in with the idea of heat. I also wanted dreadlocks, but nobody else wanted them, so we did these really great

pre-Raphaelite curls. They were concerned that a girl on another show had red hair, so they wanted blonde, but that didn't look as good. We put more and more red in until it ended up being that sort of gingery hair she has now."

Red hair clearly hadn't got out of Elsey's system when he came to create the Veneks in '…Different Destinations'. "I gave the Venek leader ginger hair, because it made him look more ferocious," he recalls. "The characters had to have some nobility, and I thought it would be a great opportunity to do some sort of Lion Men. I wanted General Grynes to have a kind of Sean Connery look about him as well."

One of the season's most important guest characters was Xhalax Sun, played by Linda Cropper. "I knew she had no problems wearing make-up," Elsey says, "as she had been a Plokavian in 'The Ugly Truth'. As soon as we heard the description of Aeryn's mum as a 'soldier with an ugly scar', we knew that we would have to create some horrible scarring at some point."

The scarring wasn't visible in the character's first appearance in 'Thanks for Sharing', and viewers had to wait for 'Relativity' before seeing the full extent of the make-up. "Colin Ware sculpted that, and he decided

Opposite page: Shane Briant as Kaarvok.

Above: The leonine Venek leader, Colonel Lennok.

Next page: Crichton encounters the Strannat.

Page 143: A Colarta tracker.

to burn off half of her face from the ear backwards," Elsey explains. "Instead of having scars like slashes, she had a laser burn."

'Thanks for Sharing' also saw the creation of the truth-seeking Strannat. "Ricky Manning told me that he needed something that if you don't tell it the truth, it'll kill you," Elsey remembers. "I asked how, and he said he didn't know. 'You make it and I'll write it!' he told me. So we had enormous difficulty. I had the idea that you put it on the top of your head, and if you told a lie it would sink two tubes into your head and suck out all your blood. It would squirt out about eight pints of blood instantly. But I was the only person who liked that, so that was put to one side."

The final creature partially resembled the face-hugger from Ridley Scott's classic movie *Alien*. "It's a crab-like thing, with a tail with a spike on the end that gets closer and closer," Elsey says. "If you start to tell lies, the spike goes straight into your forehead and brain, and you're instantly killed. That way we didn't have to show too much blood."

The trackers employed by Xhalax Sun also appeared at the end of the episode. "Nobody knew how to do the transformation," Elsey recalls. "Nobody wanted to do a CGI morph — I wanted to do a transformation with more Eighties-style effects. We built heads with bladders in them so

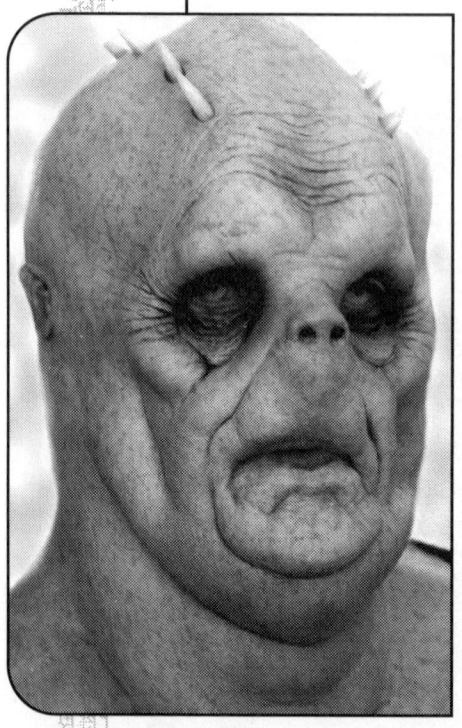

they could thrash around and stretch out, and then reveal a lizardy, snakey kind of creature which would shake off the remnants of the skin."

Other regular characters made their first appearance in 'Losing Time', as we met Scorpius's scientific team. Linfer and Co-Kura were played by Johanna Kerrigan and Danny Adcock, both of whom had previously worked on the show. "That cut a lot of time off, because we had the lifecasts of them already," Elsey explains. "With Jo, I wanted to do something really different — very human, but very minimalist, which showed a lot of her face. Her make-up was beautiful — she had more tattoos at first, but I was very pleased with the way it turned out. And then by contrast, poor old Danny got to be buried under feet of latex again!"

Adcock had previously played the blind Traltixx in 'Crackers Don't Matter' for which his lifecast had to be taken in an unusual position. "His head was leaning back a bit, to allow him room to see as Traltixx, because that make-up used a kind of periscope device," Elsey says. "This time, I thought it would be perfect to give him a double chin, because when he puts his head down, it would all squish up. Dominic Hailstone had just finished work on *Harry Potter* and was sculpting for me on *Farscape*. He shifted all the proportions around, and made tiny teeth and contact lenses that made Danny's eyes look really small."

When the actor smiled for the first time in the make-up, "everyone fell about laughing. Because of the way the features had been distorted, every time he smiled, it made him look hilarious. Danny clocked that instantly and made it part of the character. When they told me that Danny's character was going to be in the show an awful lot, I realised that I'd put him into something that he would never be able to get out of, that would be torture for him every day. But he doesn't ever complain — I think he gets a kick out of it!"

One of Elsey's favourite episodes of the season was 'Incubator'. "We couldn't wait to do an episode about Scorpy where we find out a little bit more about him," he recalls. "We had to do a child Scorpy and a young Scorpy, and it was decided that Wayne would play the young one, who would look like a very crude version of how we see him now. Basically we

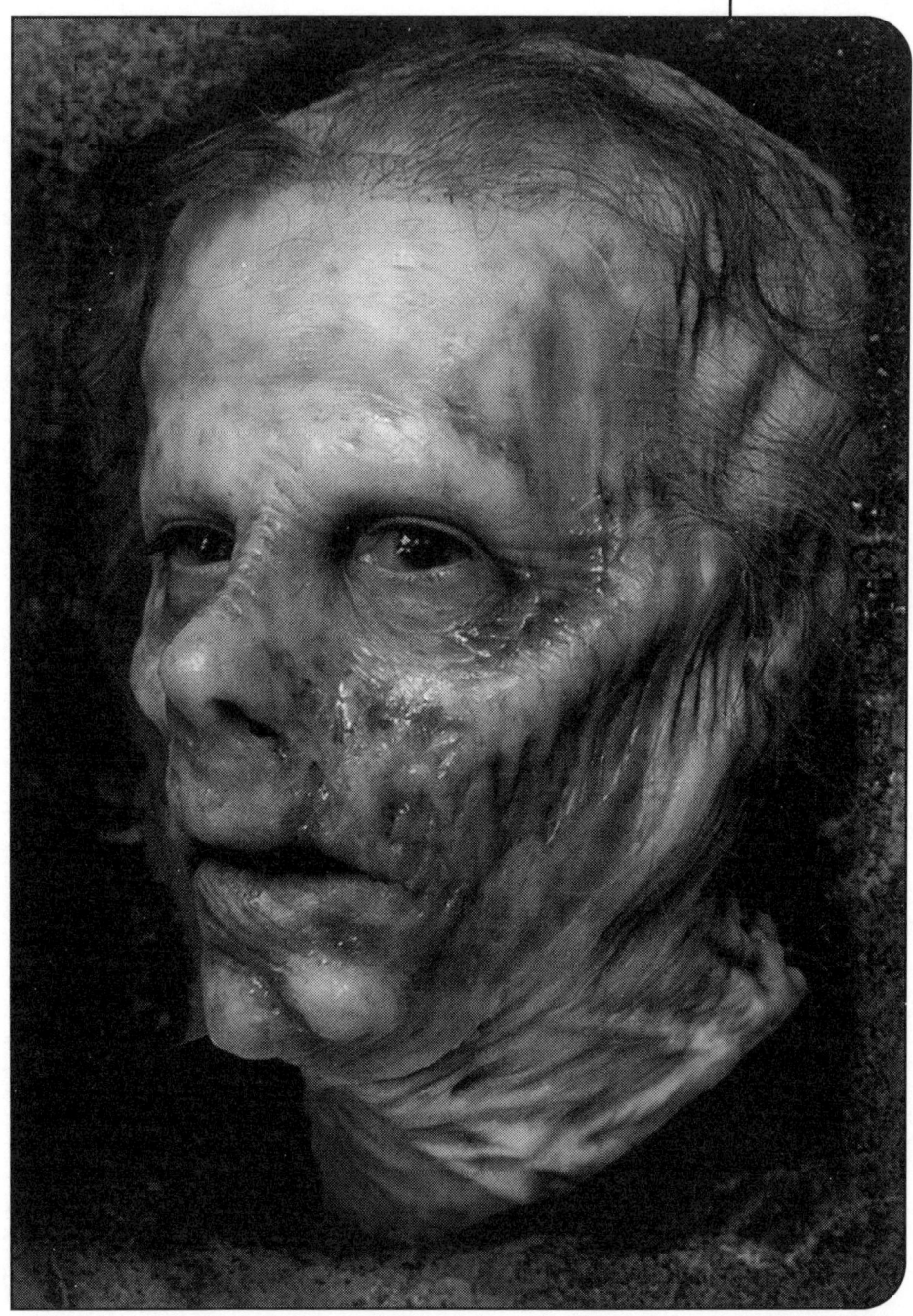

felt that the Scorpy we know and love, or hate, now is the best he's ever looked. He's at the peak of his powers — he's perfected his coolant rods and everything. When he was younger, he was a freak, and you should feel sorry for him when you first see him. So we redid his usual costume — we made it cruder, and he had to have a huge backpack with big coolant rods to cool him down. He also had a lot of scarring on his face which hadn't quite healed."

Elsey also enjoyed creating the infant Scorpius. "That's him at his worst — he shouldn't have lived. He should never have even been born," he points out. "They hired Evan Sheaves, who was very similar to Wayne — he looked like a young version of him. We pushed everything out, and made it more skeletal. We were pushing the thin aspect of it, and keeping him bound, so there was the impression that his clothing was almost keeping his body together. We had great contact lenses made for him — we wanted his eyes to look as though he had been crying all his life, so the lenses made his eyes look really blood-

shot and misted over. It was also the first time we had done a full head in Hot Flesh make-up [the special translucent compound pioneered by the Creature Shop], so Evan had to endure a lot to be inside that. I thought he gave a really good performance."

The design that ended up being used for the Hangi in 'Scratch 'n' Sniff' was originally intended for Francesca Buller as Raxil. "I wanted to give Francesca an easy time this time, because it was such a full-on make-up that we did for her as M'Lee in 'Bone to be Wild'," Elsey explains. "I designed a bondage outfit in line with the sex planet, but David said that Francesca loved going into the prosthetics, so that's what we did. Then David gave me a note during a meeting one day saying that he wanted less bipedal aliens, less of the 'two arms, two legs and a head', and he asked if we could do something like that for the Hangi, this alien that could see into other rooms. Maybe it could have a million eyes or something. I thought that was a great idea, so I redesigned what Fran had been going to wear into this other creature. It had spider legs sticking out, and there was no way that a human being could sit inside it, or get inside it in any way. It's also obviously not just a hand puppet — nobody has got their arm up it. It's completely controlled from beneath the little pedestal that it's sat on — cables come out of the back, and the face is all computer

Page 144: *Danny Adcock as Co-Kura Strappa.*

Page 145: *The infant Scorpius make-up.*

Opposite page: *A Charrid, as seen in 'Infinite Possibilities'.*

Above: *The Seer, from 'The Choice'.*

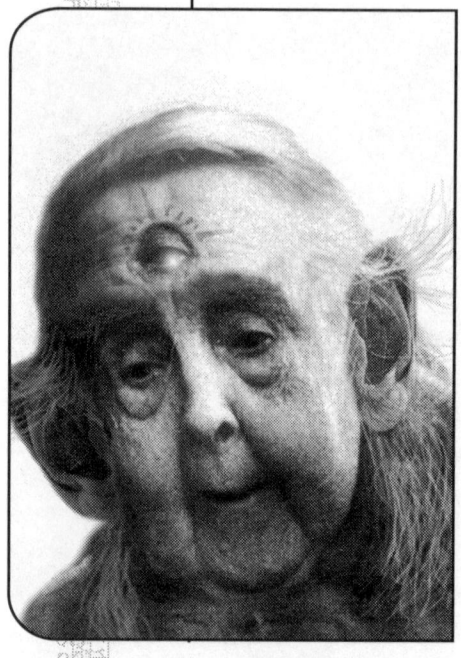

controlled. Originally, the tentacles that hung down the back of his head, Bob Marley style, were all going to be mechanical and move around like snakes, but I was worried that you wouldn't be able to tell what you were looking at. I was really pleased with the way it turned out though."

The next two-parter, 'Infinite Possibilities', saw the introduction of the Charrids. Elsey explains their genesis: "Scarrans are very expensive creatures to produce, and they are very complicated — far more ambitious than anybody in their right mind would attempt to do on a TV show! So we needed to have aliens that were maybe in alliance with the Scarrans, who we could see in larger quantities. I wanted to do creatures that were reminiscent of the Scarrans but were also very fantasy-oriented.

"The starting point for the Charrids was putting the biggest pair of false teeth into the actors' mouths that I could possibly fit in, and work from there," he continues. "That brought their faces out quite a long way, and I realised this gave me a chance to 'carve in' and get really great cheekbones, and a skeletal look. It would be reminiscent of Scorpius and the Scarrans, and you could see how they all tied up together. They also have individual tattoos on their foreheads. Actually," he reveals, "all the people who worked on them tattooed their initials onto the Charrids!"

Elsey had an encounter with another actor from a production he admired when John Gregg was cast as Talyn in 'The Choice'. "John had been in 'The Ark in Space' with Tom Baker's *Doctor Who*, and we had a ball making him up, and hearing his stories of working with Tom," Elsey recalls. "'The Choice' was a really dark episode, and it turned out to be a really scary make-up too. Martin Rizzard did an absolutely astounding job of coming up with this bizarre look for Talyn. The mutated effect was quite eerie — it might have come off as really quite silly, as a lot of these things can do if they're seen in a different light, but it worked magnificently."

Also in that episode was the Seer. "All they told me was that there would be a box, with a head in it!" Elsey reveals. "I knew we could do better than that — although Rowan Woods thought the idea of the box was brilliant and simple. My ideas are always nightmarishly complicated... So I designed this baby, and the 'box' as well — I wanted it to open like a flower, and be as interesting as we could make it. I was very pleased with that — that was the first thing that Mario Halouvas has ever taken the lead in puppeteering in the show, and he did such a great job that I can't wait to give him something else to puppeteer."

The final episode of the season introduced a mysterious Old Woman, who is still on Moya when the Leviathan vanishes through the wormhole into the start of the fourth year. "My grounding is in English children's television, and I see her as a female Catweazle [an eccentric 11th century wizard character in an early 1970s series]," Elsey says of the as-yet-unnamed character. "I wanted an alien look, but again they wanted it not to look too different to the actress. Yoda's name was mentioned amongst many other things. I got very humanistic towards the end of the season, just wanting to play with the proportions of the face. I also had the idea of doing a third eye, because I thought that would be something that the writers would be able to find some way of using, and it would become an important part of her. I wanted to do it better than it's been done

elsewhere — it's very difficult to get an eye mechanism, which can blink on someone's forehead and not have the forehead bulging right out. She's got these big ears too, which was funny, because she can't hear! We did a make-up test, and then Andrew Prowse came in with a whole list of suggestions to make her better, all of which we incorporated. If it was good before, it was a thousand times better after Andrew Prowse's suggestions!"

Elsey finds inspiration wherever he can. "I'm a terrible fanboy," he admits. "I'm a huge science fiction fan, and I'm a huge horror fan and a huge character actor fan. And I like fantasy too! I don't see any reason in a world like *Farscape*, where the stories dip into so many areas, why the make-ups have to be along a certain line all the time. I like the idea that we can go to different planets with different looks. Sometimes I take it in a fantasy direction, sometimes towards gothic horror, other times towards sci-fi — whichever seems to fit.

"I do like the darker episodes — the slightly more evil, gothic ones like 'Eat Me'. I think everything got into its stride with that episode," he concludes. "I liked Vek and Kek, the trackers from 'Relativity' — they were nice, un-TV looking aliens. And the Seer in 'The Choice' — I've never seen *anything* like that on television, and afterwards people said it reminded them of Kuato from *Total Recall*. That was a huge budget Paul Verhoeven movie with special effects by Rob Bottin. If we can get likened to something like that, then we aren't doing too badly!" ∎

Opposite page and above: Early designs for the mysterious Old Woman introduced in 'Dog with Two Bones'.

" *Farscape* is such a terrific joy for me to work on as a composer because there are these huge emotional gear changes."

hen it comes to composing for *Farscape*, my approach tends to be very functional," maintains Guy Gross, who has been writing the music for the series since a third of the way through the second year. "I score the way that I expect the audience to feel, or the way that we would *like* them to feel. With a few exceptions — like Aeryn's death — I generally make music a secondary feature. I put it smack bang where it belongs to help tell the story. If you cut the dialogue and sound effects out, and just listened to the music, a fair whack of it would be a little pedestrian perhaps, yet its use is hopefully spot on for the sequence it's required for..." The composer breaks off and grins. "Of course, when there are moments that need the music to fly and be featured, then I let out all the stops and off I go!"

"Guy doesn't just come along and put music with what we've done on screen," David Kemper adds. "He enhances it. He elevates the mood of a scene. He seems to know instinctively where the heart of a scene is, which character to follow, and he puts that up there."

The classically trained Australian composer joined the show in late 1999, making his mark with the lush score for 'The Way We Weren't'. By the end of the second season, Gross had proved that he could handle the pace and differing demands of the series, and agreed to score every episode of the third year. He was also commissioned to re-envisage the show's opening theme.

"I had a reasonably long lead time to prepare something," he recalls, "but nothing accurate in terms of brief, other than a composer's worst nightmare that 'we want something the same but different'. David Kemper eventually explained that season three would be much more

dangerous — there's a lot more at stake. So there's a lot more raw darkness in the new theme that I've done, which is essentially a co-write between me and Subvision." The theme is credited to 'Guy Gross, adapted from the original theme by Subvision', and Gross feels this is an accurate description of the music that is "somewhat familiar to the audience, yet moved away enough to be fresh. Everyone was really chuffed that it kept the spirit, yet progressed in a slightly darker way."

Gross is very conscious of the responsibility that rests on the composer's shoulders. "We have such control over the perception of a scene," he explains, thinking back to moments in 'Suns and Lovers'. "There was a reasonably long dialogue scene between D'Argo and Jothee, where the score could tip it either way. The audience could have great sympathy for these two men who should be getting along, or the music can reinforce the anger that they have for one another. I get a great kick out of moving things emotionally, especially under dialogue. Like a good, classic feature film, *Farscape* is not afraid to underscore dialogue, which a lot of Australian productions fear, because men have trouble expressing emotions, and producers don't think that dialogue should ever be laced with emotion. I try to pivot the music on every word, and every body movement. I try to follow the choreography of a scene: if characters are moving towards each other, or they've paused, you'll find that my music starts and stops with them."

Opposite page: Guy Gross in his recording studio.

Above: An angry D'Argo.

With a long sequence such as Zhaan's death, Gross sees it as his duty to help give the scene shape. "The saving grace was that she was such a religious character," he recalls, "so I could go pretty ethereal and choral. I let the audience know when they could take a breath, when she was moving on to the next chapter in this death."

Gross would rather work on an emotion-laden scene than an action sequence. "Action moments are difficult to do," he explains. "They require a lot of planning to make the action flow, and have highs and lows at the correct spots. Action music also tends to be somewhat derivative; it has to be, because it's got to have a pulse to it, to assist the drama. By virtue of its functional nature, it can sometimes be less creative than the emotional scenes."

There are also moments when the music becomes the focus of the scene. Gross quickly established that many of the sequences in 'Wolf in Sheep's Clothing' came under this heading. "Musically, we were letting the audience know the enormity of what was going on," he says. "I had a massed male choir and a full symphony orchestra banging away on the soundtrack — even if in reality it was only twelve singers and a whole bunch of samplers, it still sounded pretty huge! That episode is probably the best

example of the wide variety of styles that *Farscape* calls upon musically, and it calls upon them in very quick succession. As soon as the stand-off between John and Scorpius at the end comes to a close, we suddenly go into a Crichton/Aeryn scene. We go from this huge symphonic movement to a very gentle oboe and piano moment. I couldn't go from bigger to smaller if I tried."

Gross's innovative work on season three received acclaim from the prestigious Australian Guild of Screen Composers in December 2001, when he won the 'Best Music for an Animation' Screen Award for his score for 'Revenging Angel'. It was well-deserved recognition for the composer, who loves sitting in his studio in the post-production facility on the Fox lot, underpinning the journey of Moya's crew. "It's the joy of *Farscape* that they don't hold back," he explains. "They are happy to make huge gear changes, and they do them so confidently and so well. Every department follows that brief so nicely that it's pretty much always achieved with great confidence. If you listen to just the music, it shows why *Farscape* is such a blast for me as a composer to work on. I don't know if they created this series just so I could have fun, but it certainly seems that way sometimes!" ∎

Opposite page: Aeryn and the Seer in 'The Choice', another emotion-laden scene enhanced by Gross's accompaniment.

Above: *Gross working on the music for Aeryn's resurrection in 'Season of Death'.*

INTO SEASON FOUR

David Kemper

"Next year will have a different tone. We have set some things in motion – our characters are not going to make the same mistakes again. This year had darkness, but *Farscape*'s like life: a year later and you could be on top of the world..."

"Each week, *Farscape*'s mixture of humour and drama, and its richness of character and theme are a delight. Ben Browder, as the displaced space traveller, plays serious scenes as well as he plays comedy, and he plays comedy superbly. The entire cast is multi-talented." *The New York Daily News* heralded the arrival of *Farscape*'s first East Coast American convention with this review of the series, echoing the words of critics across the world, as the third season of the show continued to gain new fans.

Farscape was also acclaimed by the professional science fiction community, winning a prestigious Saturn Award for Best Syndicated/Cable Television Series from the Academy of Science Fiction, Fantasy and Horror Films at their twenty-seventh annual Awards Ceremony in June 2001. "The science fiction community holds a very special place in my heart. It is a particularly thoughtful and discerning audience, so winning the Saturn is an especially gratifying experience," commented Rockne S. O'Bannon, while David Kemper added, "*Farscape* merges the best in creative talents — inventive writing, superior acting, feature-film quality visual effects, state-of-the-art creatures and animatronics, as well as award-winning make-up, costume and set design — into a series that is not afraid of taking risks." In March 2002, the series and the main cast were rewarded with five further Saturn nominations.

Tie-in merchandise proliferated. The DVDs continued to sell well, and both Contender Video in the UK and AD Vision in America worked with the *Farscape* crew to produce a wealth of extras on every disc. "We've been trying to track down concept drawings and materials," post-production supervisor Deb Peart explains. "We want to produce *Farscape* DVDs with the most amount of features, and make them really wild!"

Tor and Boxtree Books brought out further fictional adventures, while Wildstorm Comics produced a six-page special comic strip for *TV Guide*, written by comics legend Marv Wolfman, followed by a two-issue miniseries. Titan Books' second *Illustrated Companion* stood proudly on the shelves next to its predecessor, and Titan also launched a bi-monthly magazine, celebrating all aspects of the series. "The response from the readers constantly amazes me, and the amount of help from the *Farscape* production team is unbelievable," says editor Martin Eden. "Those guys are so busy

getting the show together, but they always go to extra lengths to help me out with everything I need. And David Kemper is 'The Man'! Recently, he was in the middle of working on about five different *Farscape* scripts and yet he still managed to spend time putting together his latest column for the magazine. The enthusiasm and dedication of everyone involved is astonishing."

If they so desired, fans could buy new action figures, with their favourite characters adopting poses from different episodes, adorn their walls with posters and calendars, and enjoy a tipple from *Farscape* wine glasses. A soundtrack album of musical selections from the first two seasons was released, with further CDs promised for 2002.

Two conventions were organised by Creation Entertainment in Los Angeles and New York at the start of September 2001, as post-production work on the third season drew to a close. The season's final four episodes premièred in Great Britain in January 2002, although American fans had to wait until April before discovering what would happen aboard the Command Carrier. But the best news for the fans came on 1 October 2001, when SCI FI announced that it had ordered not one, but two more seasons of *Farscape*.

Andrew Prowse stepped up to the producer's chair for the fourth year. "It seems I do three times as much work," he jokes. "It's daunting and

Above: David Kemper, Ben Browder, Ricky Manning and Carleton Eastlake pay careful attention to new producer Andrew Prowse at the 2001 Farscape convention in Burbank.

rewarding at the same time. In terms of what we're doing, I don't know that we could get any darker than the Season of Death. We've had chips in people's brains, our hero has a clone living in his head, and we've been in the hands of one of the best villains in TV history. I don't think there is much choice but to broaden our horizons and head into a lot of different and interesting places, to have new kinds of adventures. We also need to shift our villains. Some of our villains will become friends, and some of our friends will become villains! We'll surprise people that way."

Rebecca Riggs is delighted to be returning as Commandant Grayza, to become a thorn in the side of both Crichton and Scorpius. "Working on *Farscape* is extremely challenging, because they're looking for breadth and depth at the same time," she explains. "You need a scope and size of performance that isn't 'kitchen-sink-ish' at all. I'm a big sci-fi fan, so it's also a dream come true. *Farscape* is a big, grand canvas where you can discuss important issues like power, love and strength. It's a bit like Shakespeare, which I also love! Grayza is extremely strong, but I think that she might learn something else about strength from Crichton. Because she's part of a particular culture, the Peacekeeper regime, she has a very specific idea of what strength is, and what weakness is. I think Crichton might shift that in her slightly. That would be an interesting challenge for her to face."

Grayza isn't the only character to face change in the new year. "I'm excited about the new season," Claudia Black says. "David's come up with some rather interesting ideas, and Ben's writing another episode early on. I'm really looking forward to working on his script. We've got quite an exciting change coming for Aeryn in season four — it's a big deal for me! Plus, we've got a new head of make-up, who's adapted Aeryn's look slightly. We're just trying some new things. It's good to have different people coming in, as they always bring fresh ideas."

Rowan Woods hints at some incredible effects to come. "I'm just about to go into the shoot of a big double episode that's up early in the new season," he says. "If you think the water stunt in 'Wolf in Sheep's Clothing' was ambitious, just wait till you see the stunts that we are about to throw at you…" Deb Peart is equally upbeat. "The first three episodes are pretty big, and I think the results are going to be explosive," she promises. "We're now filming in widescreen. We're recutting the main title as well. If people walk away from the final episode of series three and wonder how we're going to top it, the first episode is quite a way to get into the new season."

"'Dog with Two Bones' came out of left field," David Kemper points out. "Its companion piece, the first episode of season four, has to be equally left field. The closer you get to the end of a journey, the less options you have. I already know what the end of the fourth year is," he

teases, "so I automatically know what the start of the fifth year is. And I know the end of the fifth year too!"

Kemper promises that the start of the fourth year will be "unique. Unlike anything we've ever done before. It'll be different, in a good way. I'm not familiar with any other show in the genre that's doing what we're doing. And by the middle of the season, we'll be doing a few things that people thought even *Farscape* would never do! Other shows certainly don't do them, because they're too scary. The end of the year will be marked by some very serious surprises, of the magnitude you've come to expect at the close of the season. But there will always be humour, there will always be action-adventure, and there will always be the science fiction element."

The executive producer sees the show as "like this little go-kart. People start adding things to it, and when it's all done you say, 'Johnny, that's really ugly,' and Johnny says, 'Yeah, but it's the fastest go-kart on the street.' We may be an ugly go-kart, but we're the fastest. Nobody can beat us!"

Kemper concludes by expanding Forrest Gump's adage of life being like a box of chocolates. "With season four, you're going to bite into the chocolate, pull it away from your mouth, squint at it and ask what you got. It's still *Farscape*. It's just going to taste different!" ∎

Above: Part of the growing range of Farscape *action figures.*

THE LEXICON

"I've said all along that my proudest contribution to humanity may be a new 'f' word," jokes Rockne S. O'Bannon. Here's a new A-Z selection of words that the writers of *Farscape* have contributed to humanity.

Balliun — stick, rod, pole, as in: He's really got a balliun up his butt

Blotcher — crude swear word, equivalent to bastard

Bubba — part of the slang phrase 'Deaf as a bubba'

Caritonga plague — dangerous disease of unknown origin

Chakan mist — dense layer of fog that clings to the surface of the forest planet where Talyn recuperates

Drackik — measurement of weight or heaviness: It weighs a drackik

Drexim — a synaptic fluid naturally occurring in Talyn's conduits — the Leviathan equivalent of adrenaline

Farca — fallacy, fantasy, propaganda: That's complete farca!

Fekik — planet, land, as in: Running to the ends of the fekik

Flitz — term for hell used by Furlow, as in: Unstable as all flitz

Gallian crystal — a precious gem or crystal of unknown origin

Garanzay — insurance, collateral

Graa — mark of respect, a form of address, equivalent of Sir

Grimmat — insult, equivalent of wuss or wimp

Heske — Mister (as in: Mr Crichton), a common term on the planet Lomo

I-Yensch bracelets — two bracelets that are electronically attuned to each other. When fitted to the wrists (or equivalent) of two creatures, each feels the pain of the other; if one is injured, so is the other; if one dies, both die

Javinian Poker — alien gambling game

Kasnik — equivalent of bigshot, playboy, player, used on the pleasure planet Lomo

Keehak — a beverage (like coffee) useful for sobering up drunks

Kelsa Yon — a sacred Leviathan burial region

Kretmers — currency unit

Krishool — the criminally insane

Lisch-tog — Boot-lick, tagger-on, lackey

Mallot — unit of volume or mass measurement: One tenth of a mallot

Merimar root — major ingredient in the pleasure elixirs found on the planet Lomo

Minklets — peanuts, as in: Working for minklets

Oarusk fruit — vaguely melon-shaped fruit that grows wild on the jungle planet. Its juice is highly acidic, will burn anything it touches and sizzles through most substances

Oculars — Peacekeeper issue vision/distance enhancers which work by increasing the effectiveness of the neurons of the eye

Partanium Isotope — nuclear fuel, equivalent of uranium/plutonium isotope

Rasnol — somewhat alcoholic alien drink

Rastors — a part of a being's physiological make-up, similar to genes. They are identical in direct blood relations and will show up on a basic blood test

Tak-Five torpedoes — aka 'Taks'. Missiles which have a hand-held firing mechanism, a launcher that can be operated by a single person. The actual 'warhead' of the torpedo is a fusion bonded Rhenium grabbing claw that engages upon impact, holding fast to any solid surface

Union Tattoo — Luxan symbol of courage, honour and loyalty

Valtek — equivalent of 'Freeze!' or 'Don't move!' in PK speak

Walteran Fountain — spectacular, pluming water source

Yave of the Yuvo — equivalent of 'state of the art'

Zangblats — curse word, equivalent of dammit, phooey

Zy-limbron — Banik term for limbo or purgatory